STRANGER THINGS

THE BULLY

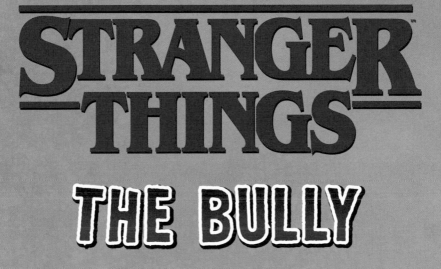

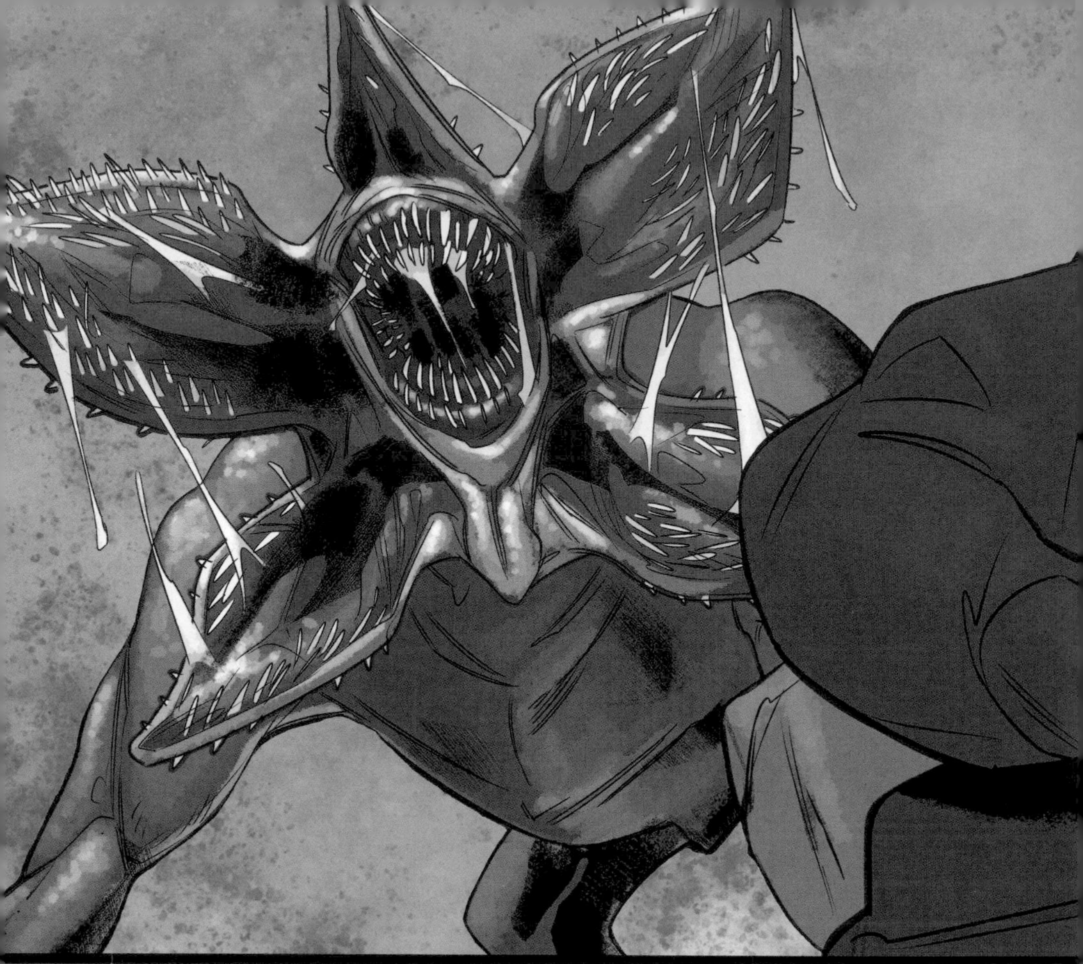

STRANGER THINGS™

THE BULLY

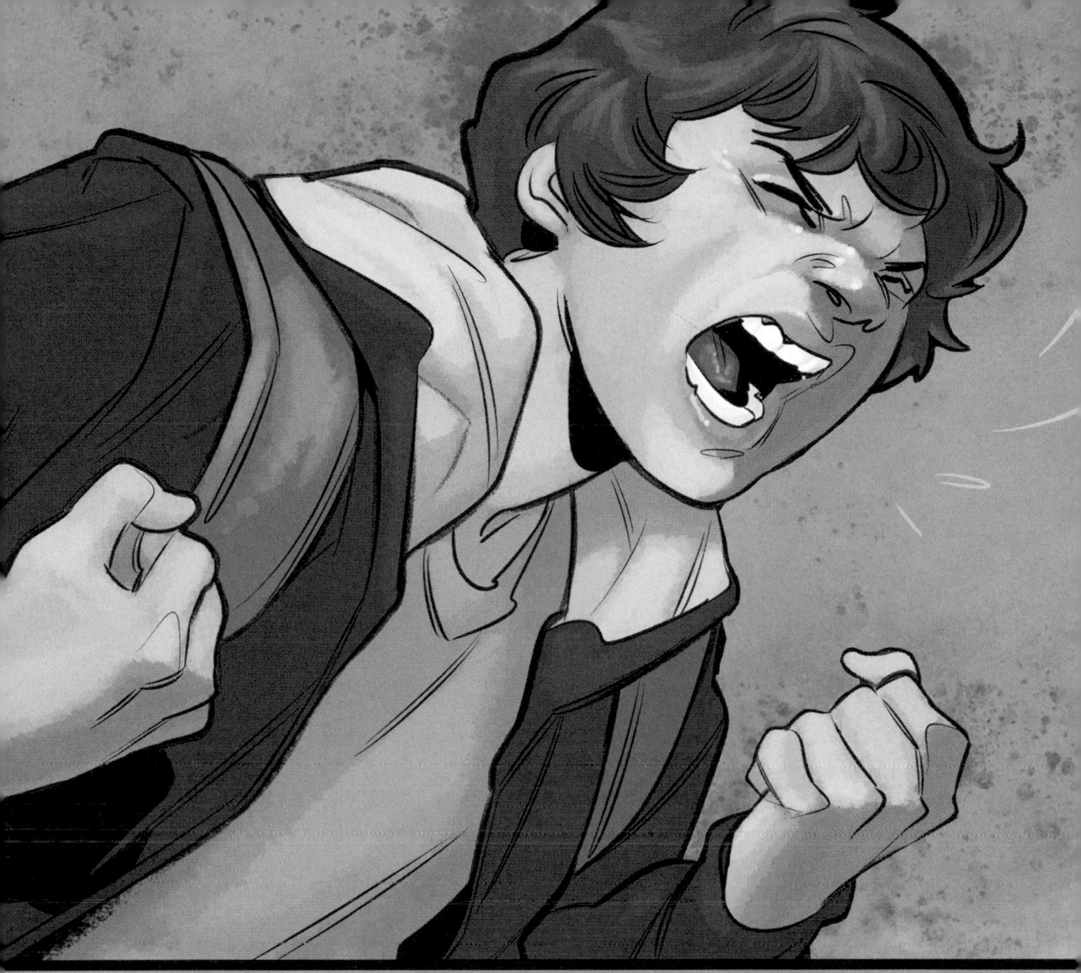

Script by
GREG PAK

Art by
VALERIA FAVOCCIA

Colors by
DAN JACKSON

Lettering by
NATE PIEKOS of **BLAMBOT**®

Cover Art by
RON CHAN

Dark Horse Books

President & Publisher
MIKE RICHARDSON

Editor
SPENCER CUSHING

Assistant Editor
KONNER KNUDSEN

Designer
PATRICK SATTERFIELD

Digital Art Technician
ALLYSON HALLER

Special thanks to Anastacia Ferry and Shannon Schram at Netflix.

Published by DARK HORSE BOOKS
A division of Dark Horse Comics LLC.
10956 SE Main Street
Milwaukie, OR 97222

DarkHorse.com | Netflix.com

First edition: August 2020
Digital ISBN 978-1-50671-503-2
ISBN 978-1-50671-453-0

10 9 8 7 6 5 4 3 2 1
Printed in Canada

To find a comics shop in your area, visit comicshoplocator.com

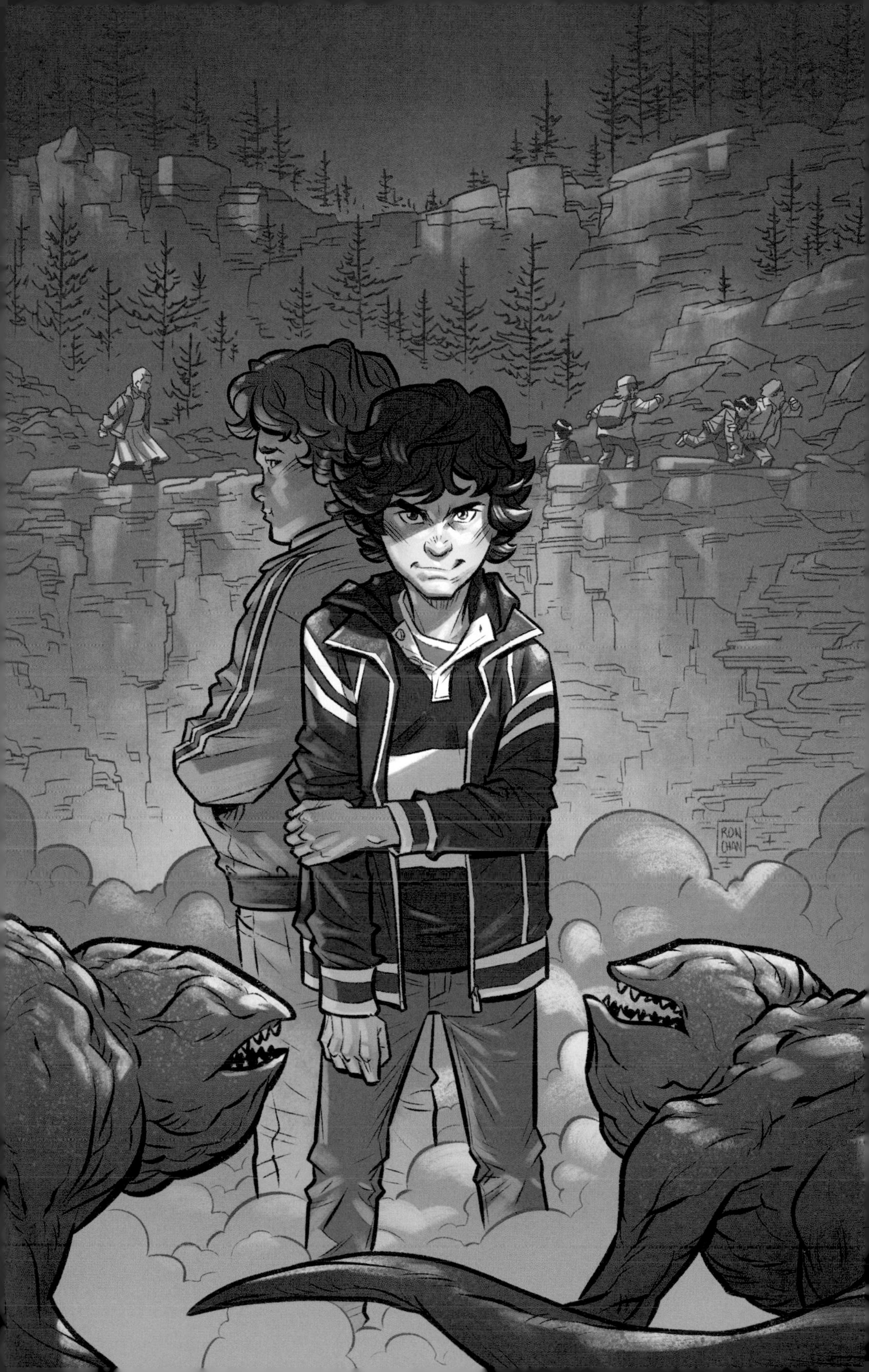
RON CHAN

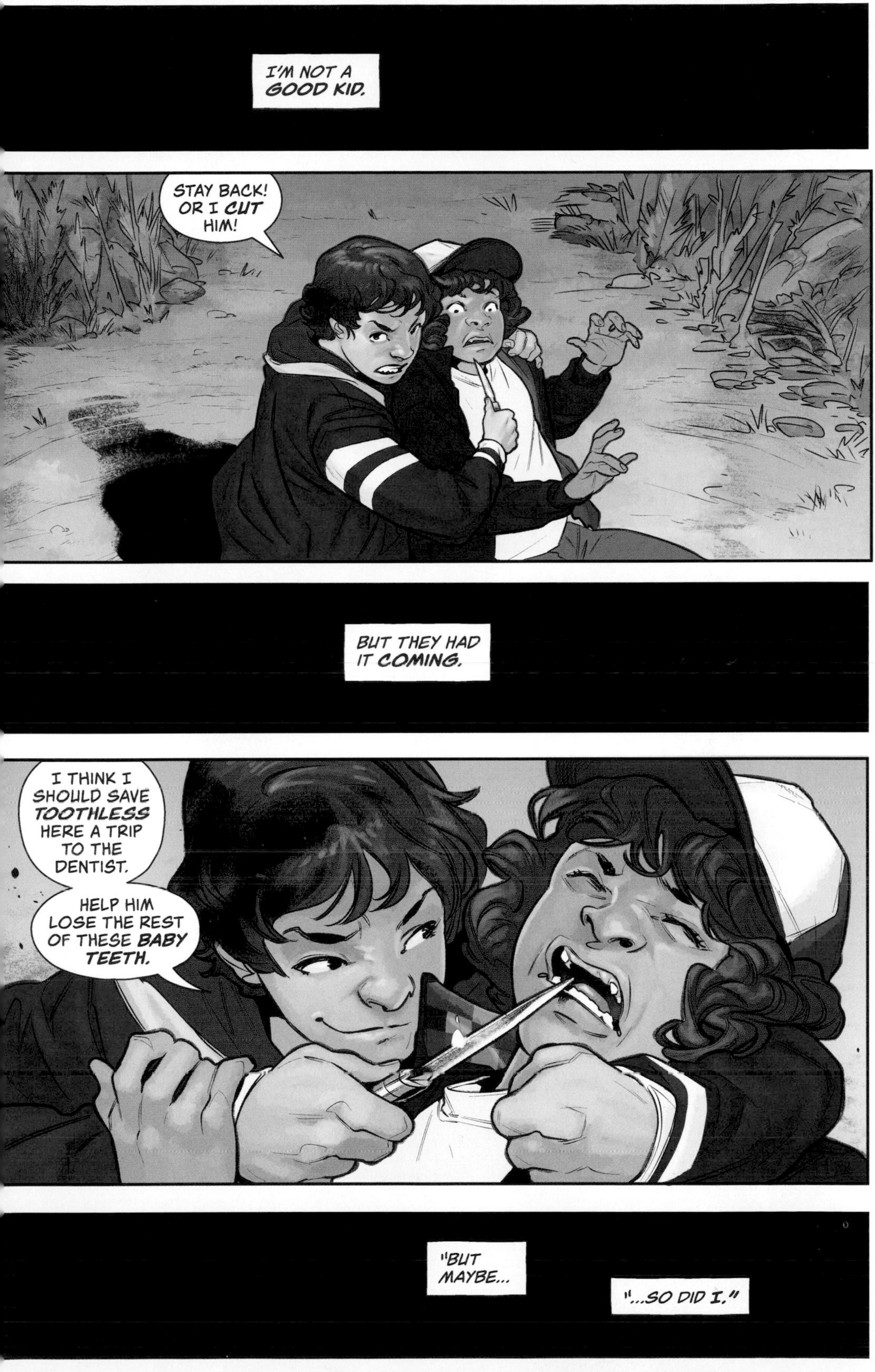
I'M NOT A GOOD KID.
STAY BACK! OR I CUT HIM!
BUT THEY HAD IT COMING.
I THINK I SHOULD SAVE TOOTHLESS HERE A TRIP TO THE DENTIST.
HELP HIM LOSE THE REST OF THESE BABY TEETH.
"BUT MAYBE...
"...SO DID I."

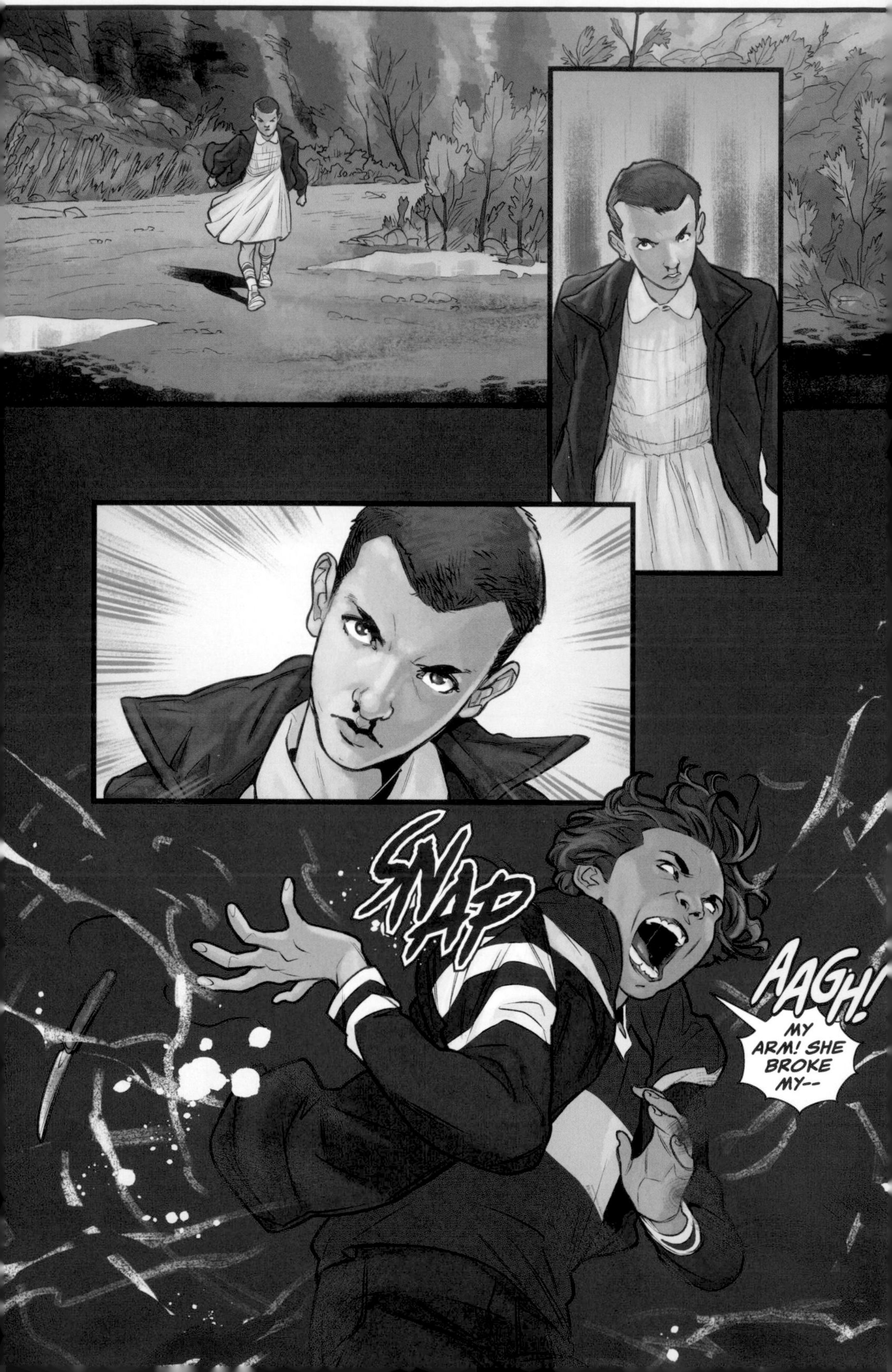
SNAP
AAGH!
MY ARM! SHE BROKE MY--

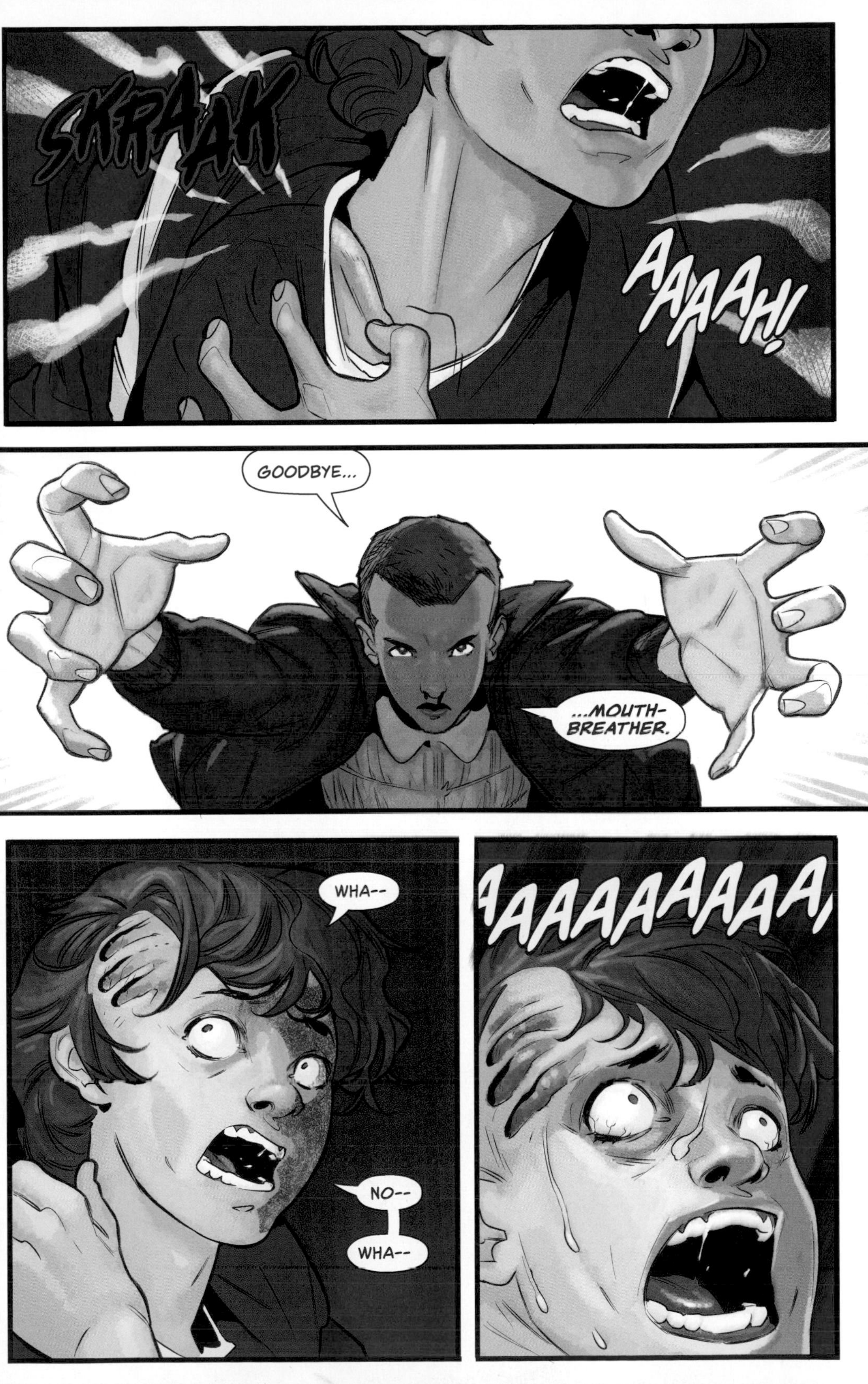
SKRAAK
AAAAH!
GOODBYE...
...MOUTH-BREATHER.
WHA--
NO--
WHA--
AAAAAAAAA

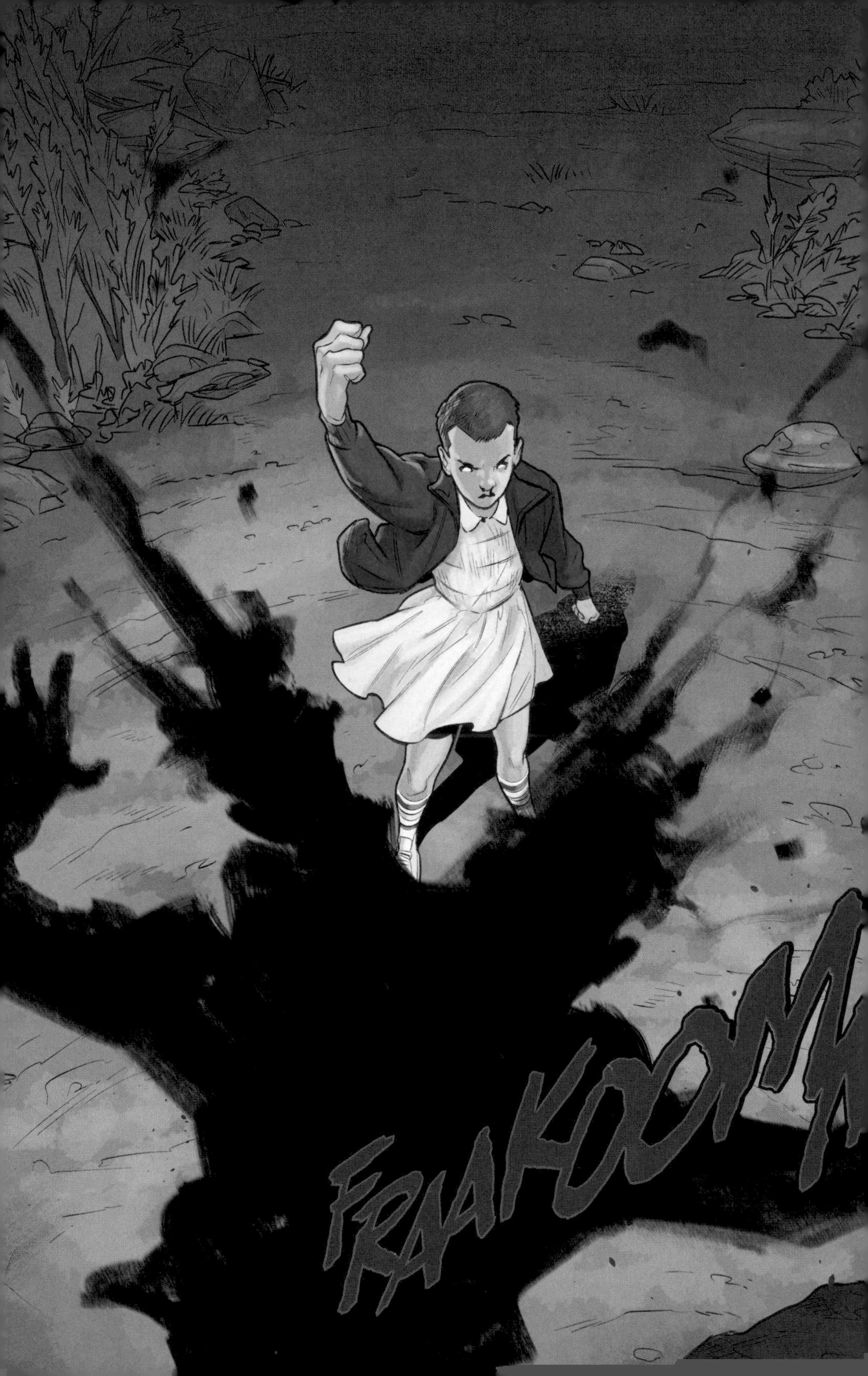
FRAAKOOM

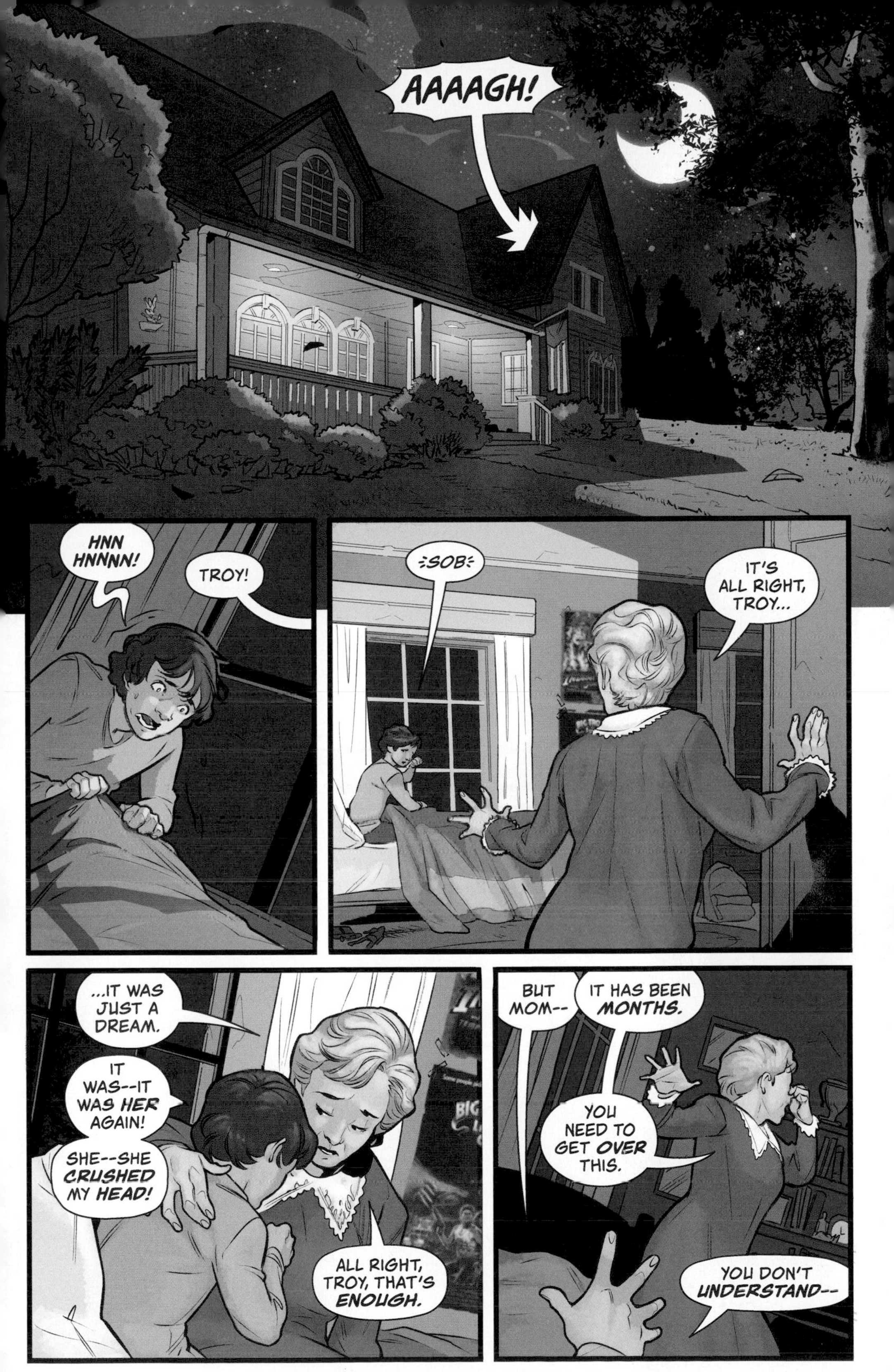
AAAAGH!
HNN HNNNN!
TROY!
SOB
IT'S ALL RIGHT, TROY...
...IT WAS JUST A DREAM.
IT WAS--IT WAS HER AGAIN!
SHE--SHE CRUSHED MY HEAD!
ALL RIGHT, TROY, THAT'S ENOUGH.
BUT MOM--
IT HAS BEEN MONTHS.
YOU NEED TO GET OVER THIS.
YOU DON'T UNDERSTAND--

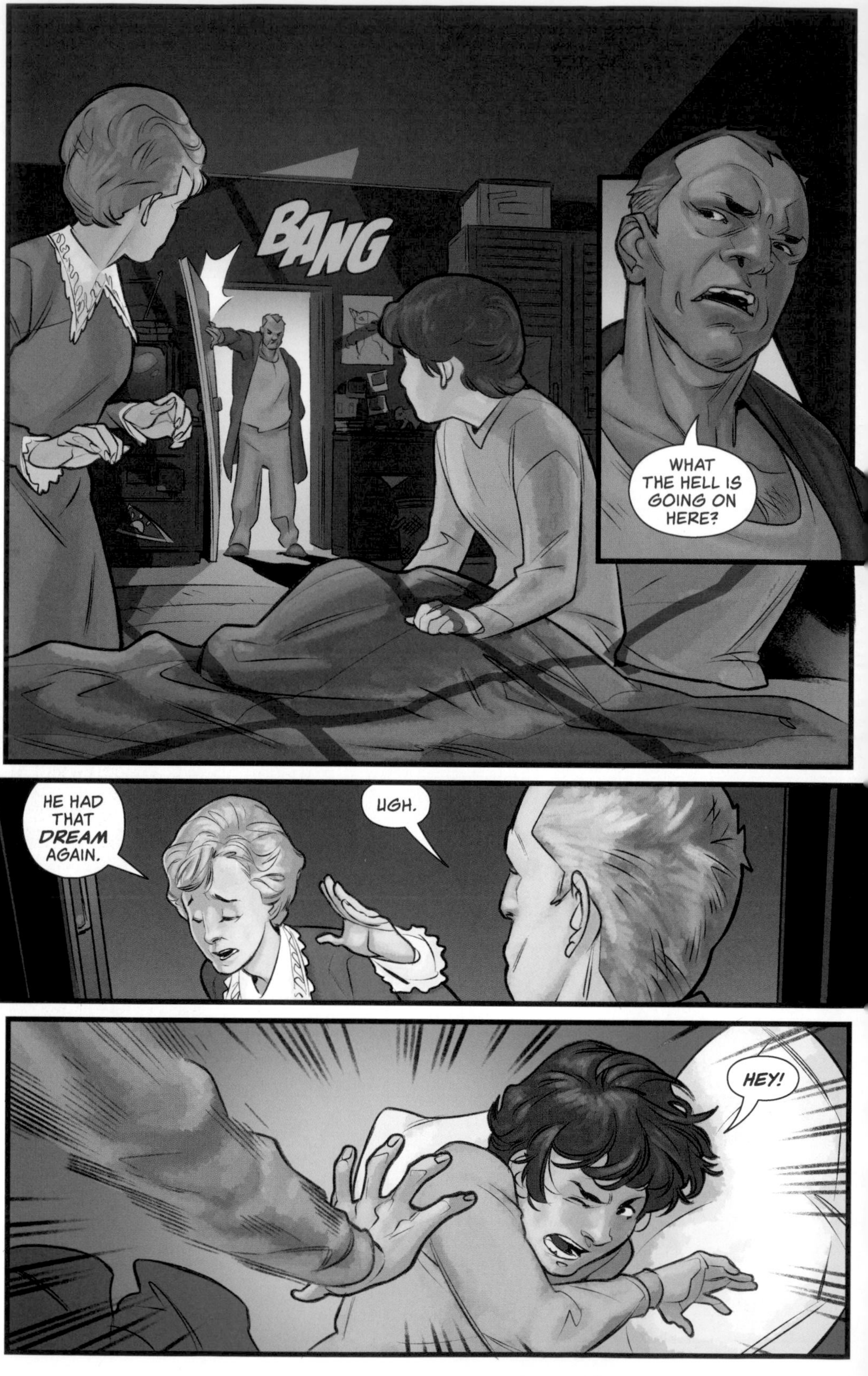
BANG
WHAT THE HELL IS GOING ON HERE?
HE HAD THAT DREAM AGAIN.
UGH.
HEY!

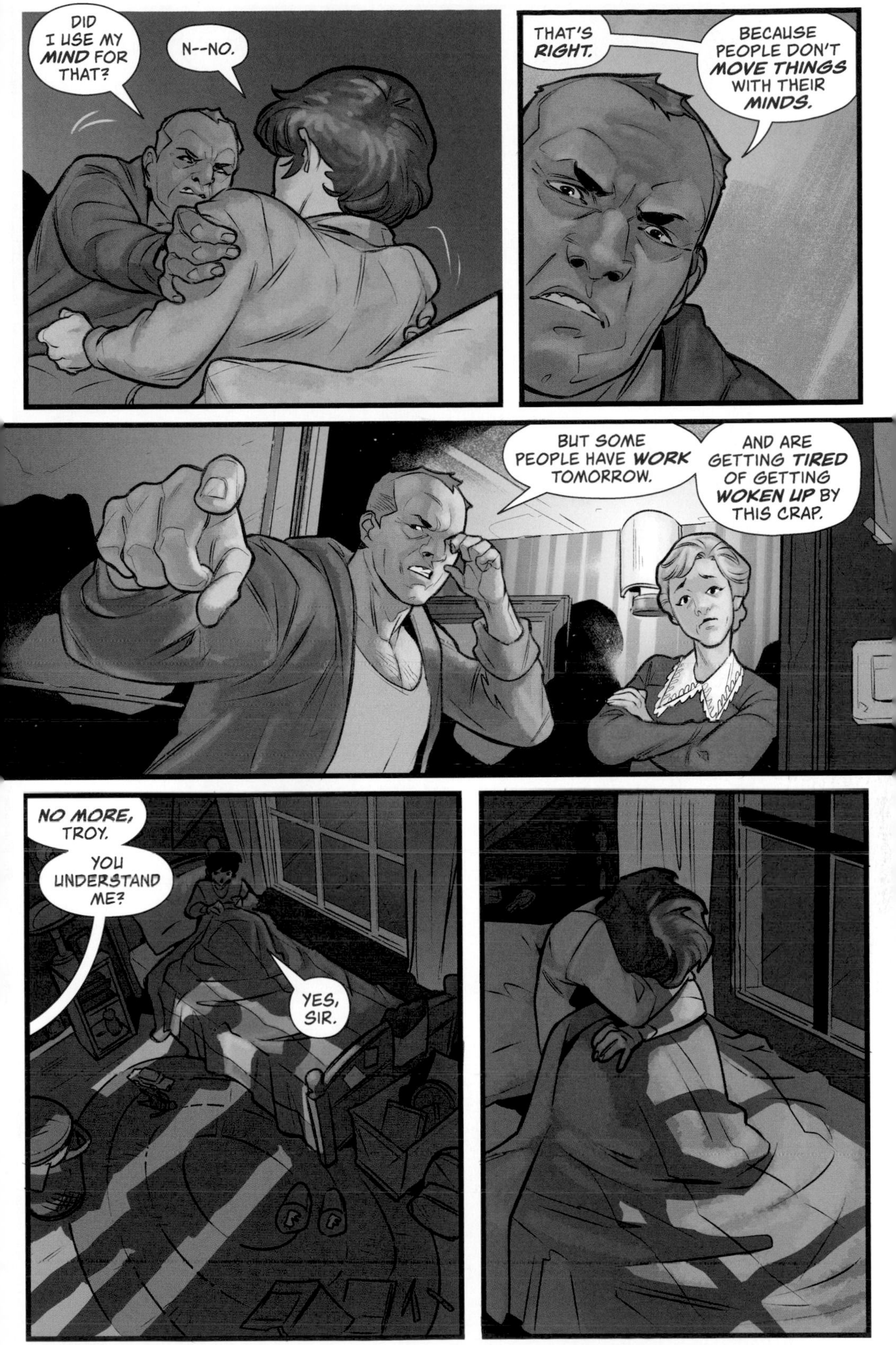
DID I USE MY MIND FOR THAT?
N--NO.
THAT'S RIGHT.
BECAUSE PEOPLE DON'T MOVE THINGS WITH THEIR MINDS.
BUT SOME PEOPLE HAVE WORK TOMORROW.
AND ARE GETTING TIRED OF GETTING WOKEN UP BY THIS CRAP.
NO MORE, TROY.
YOU UNDERSTAND ME?
YES, SIR.

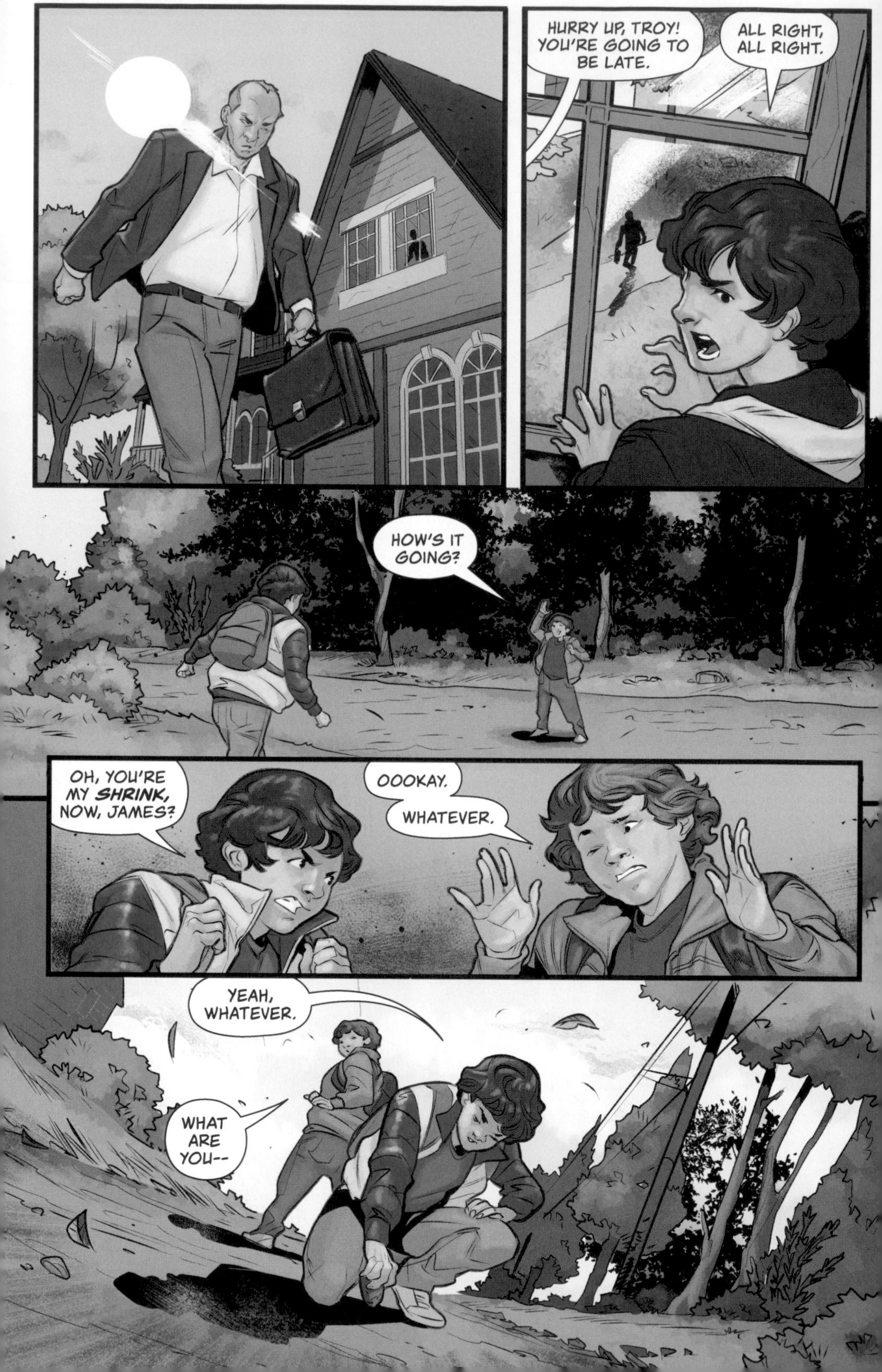
HURRY UP, TROY! YOU'RE GOING TO BE LATE.
ALL RIGHT, ALL RIGHT.
HOW'S IT GOING?
OH, YOU'RE MY *SHRINK*, NOW, JAMES?
OOOKAY.
WHATEVER.
YEAH, WHATEVER.
WHAT ARE YOU--

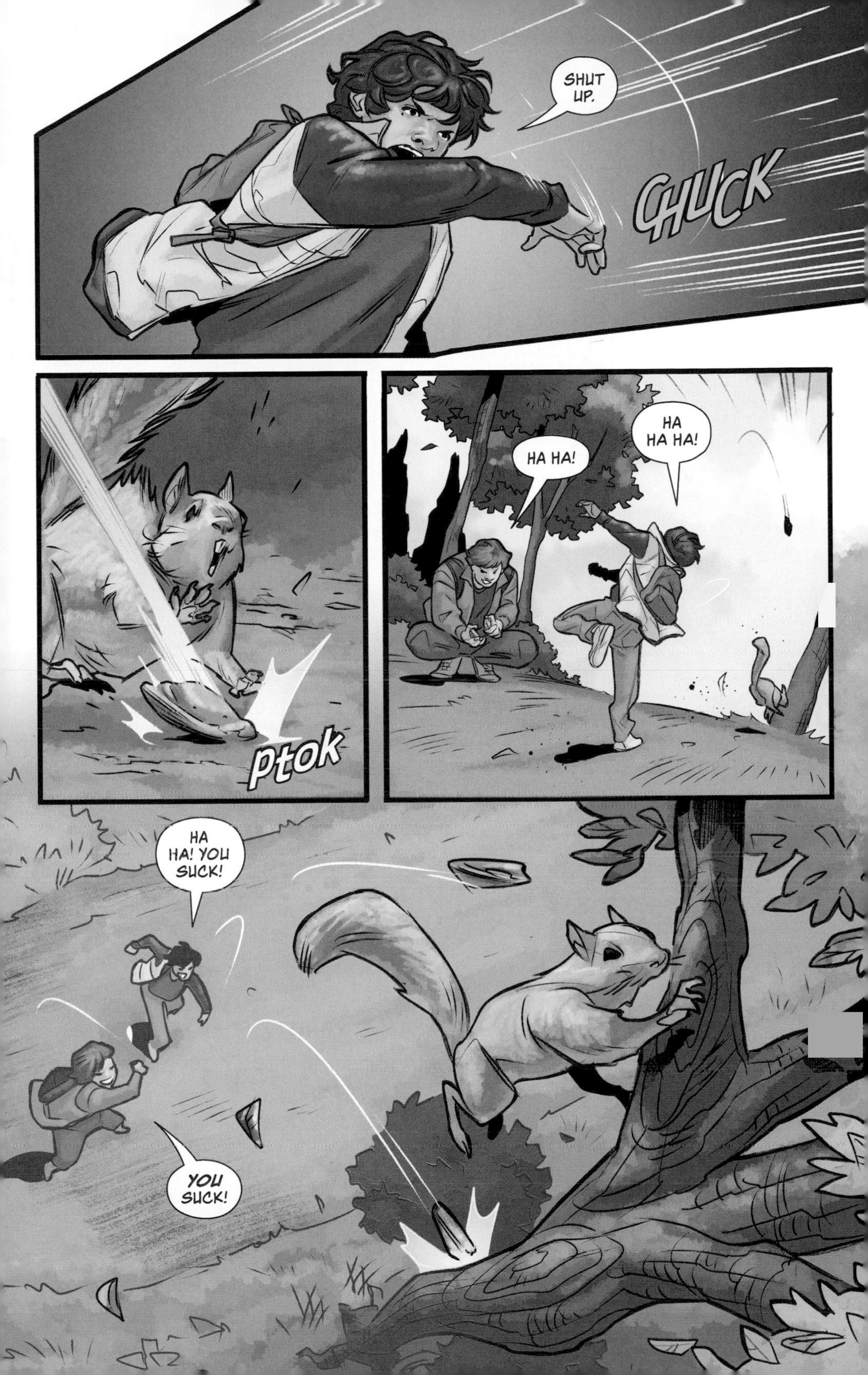
SHUT UP.
CHUCK
ptok
HA HA!
HA HA HA!
HA HA! YOU SUCK!
YOU SUCK!

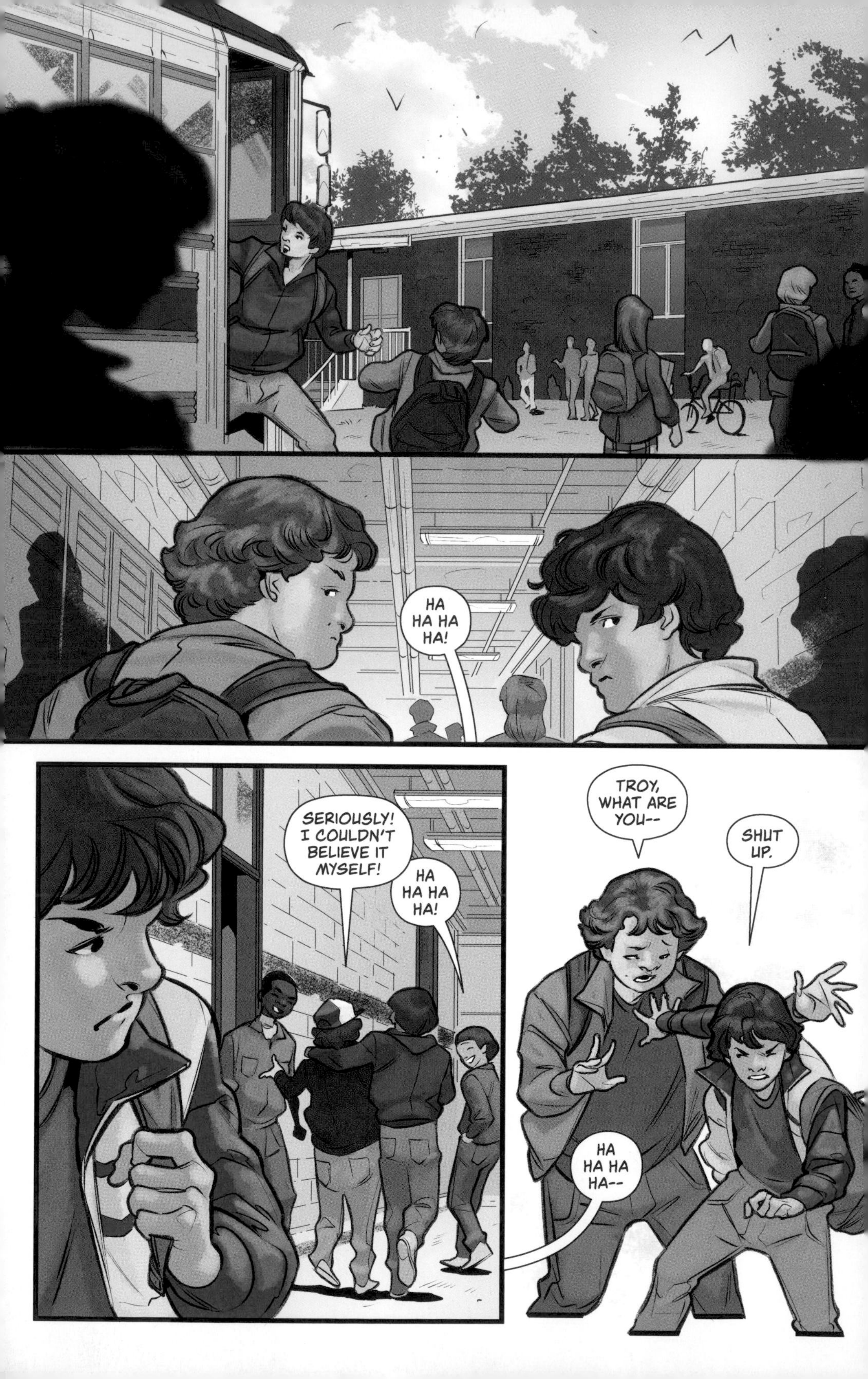
HA HA HA HA!
SERIOUSLY! I COULDN'T BELIEVE IT MYSELF!
HA HA HA HA!
TROY, WHAT ARE YOU--
SHUT UP.
HA HA HA HA--

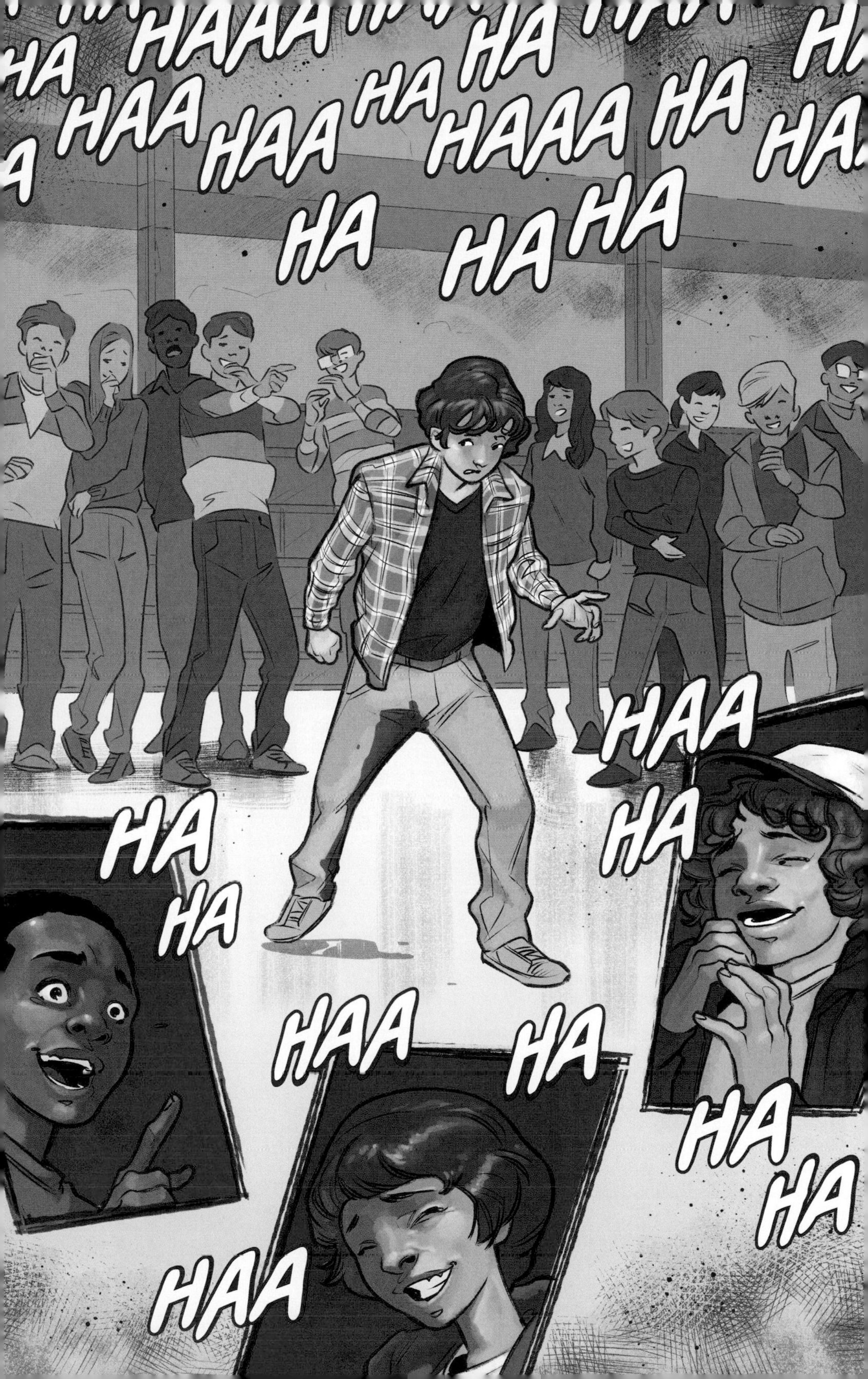
HA
HAAA
HA
HAA
HAA
HA
HAAA
HA
HA
HA
HAA
HA
HA
HA
HAA
HA
HA
HA
HAA

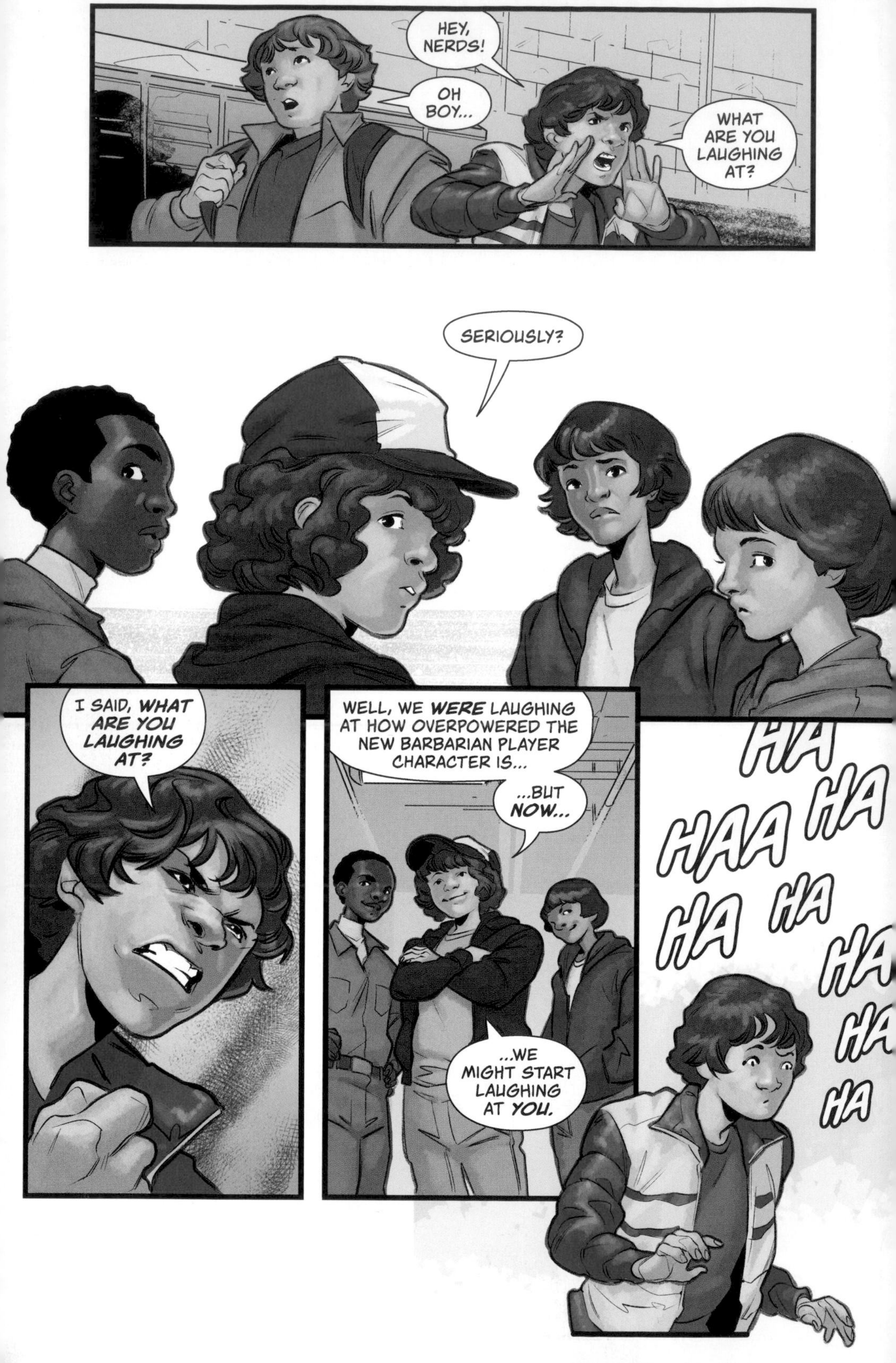
HEY, NERDS!
OH BOY...
WHAT ARE YOU LAUGHING AT?
SERIOUSLY?
I SAID, WHAT ARE YOU LAUGHING AT?
WELL, WE WERE LAUGHING AT HOW OVERPOWERED THE NEW BARBARIAN PLAYER CHARACTER IS...
...BUT NOW...
...WE MIGHT START LAUGHING AT YOU.
HA HAA HA HA HA HA HA HA HA

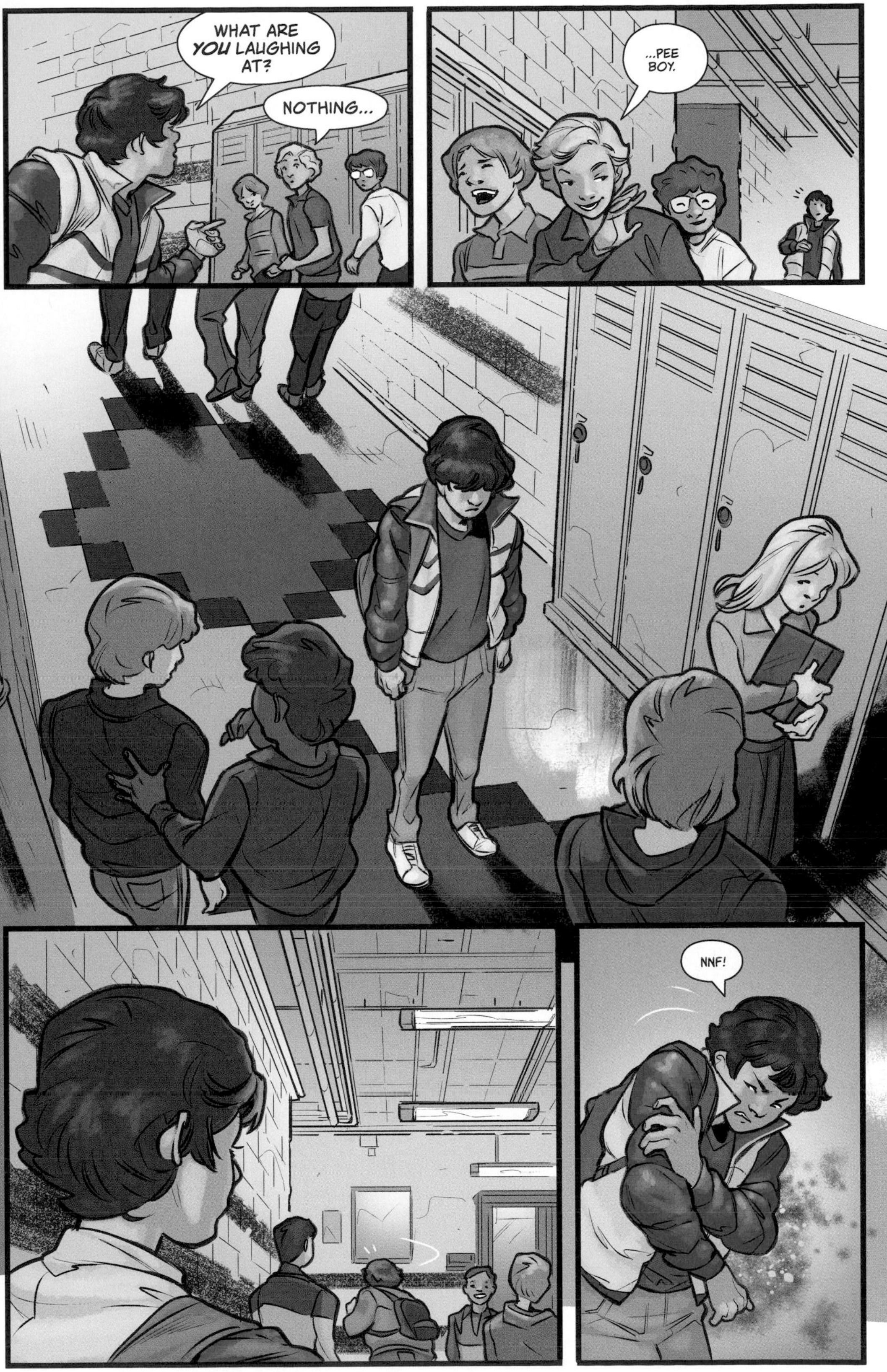
WHAT ARE YOU LAUGHING AT?
NOTHING...
...PEE BOY.
NNF!

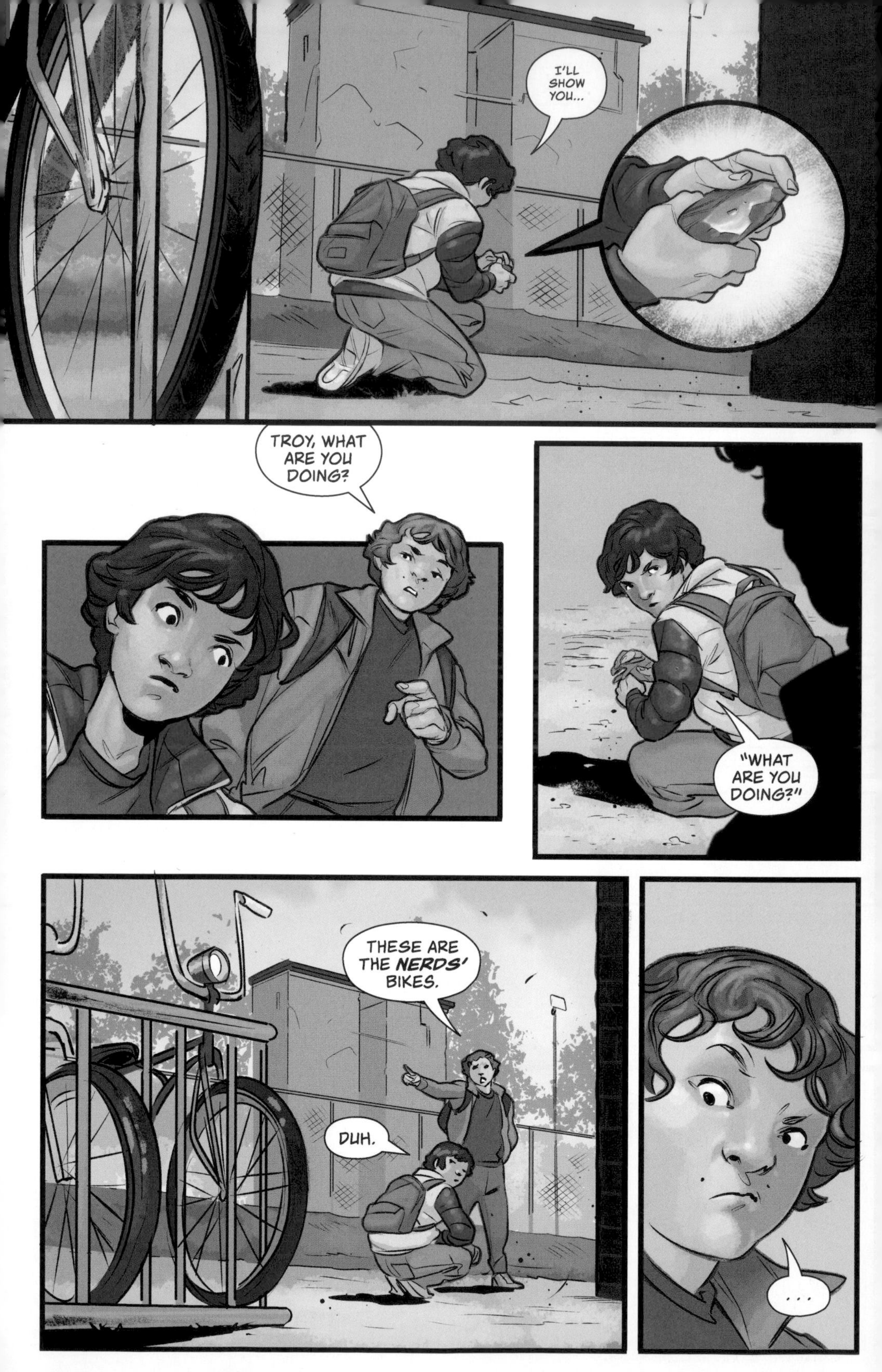
I'LL SHOW YOU...
TROY, WHAT ARE YOU DOING?
"WHAT ARE YOU DOING?"
THESE ARE THE NERDS' BIKES.
DUH.
...

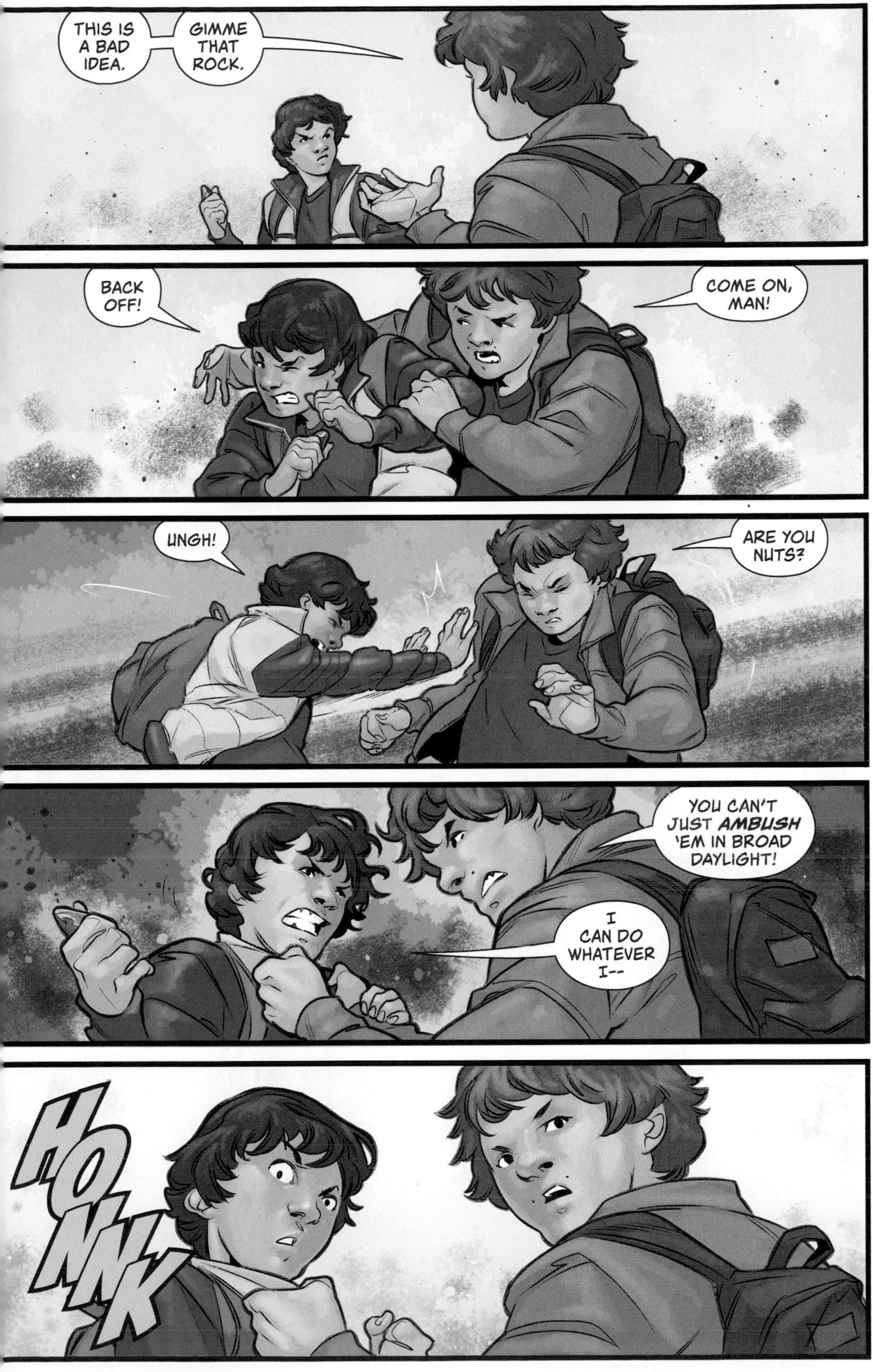
THIS IS A BAD IDEA.
GIMME THAT ROCK.
BACK OFF!
COME ON, MAN!
UNGH!
ARE YOU NUTS?
YOU CAN'T JUST AMBUSH 'EM IN BROAD DAYLIGHT!
I CAN DO WHATEVER I--
HONNK

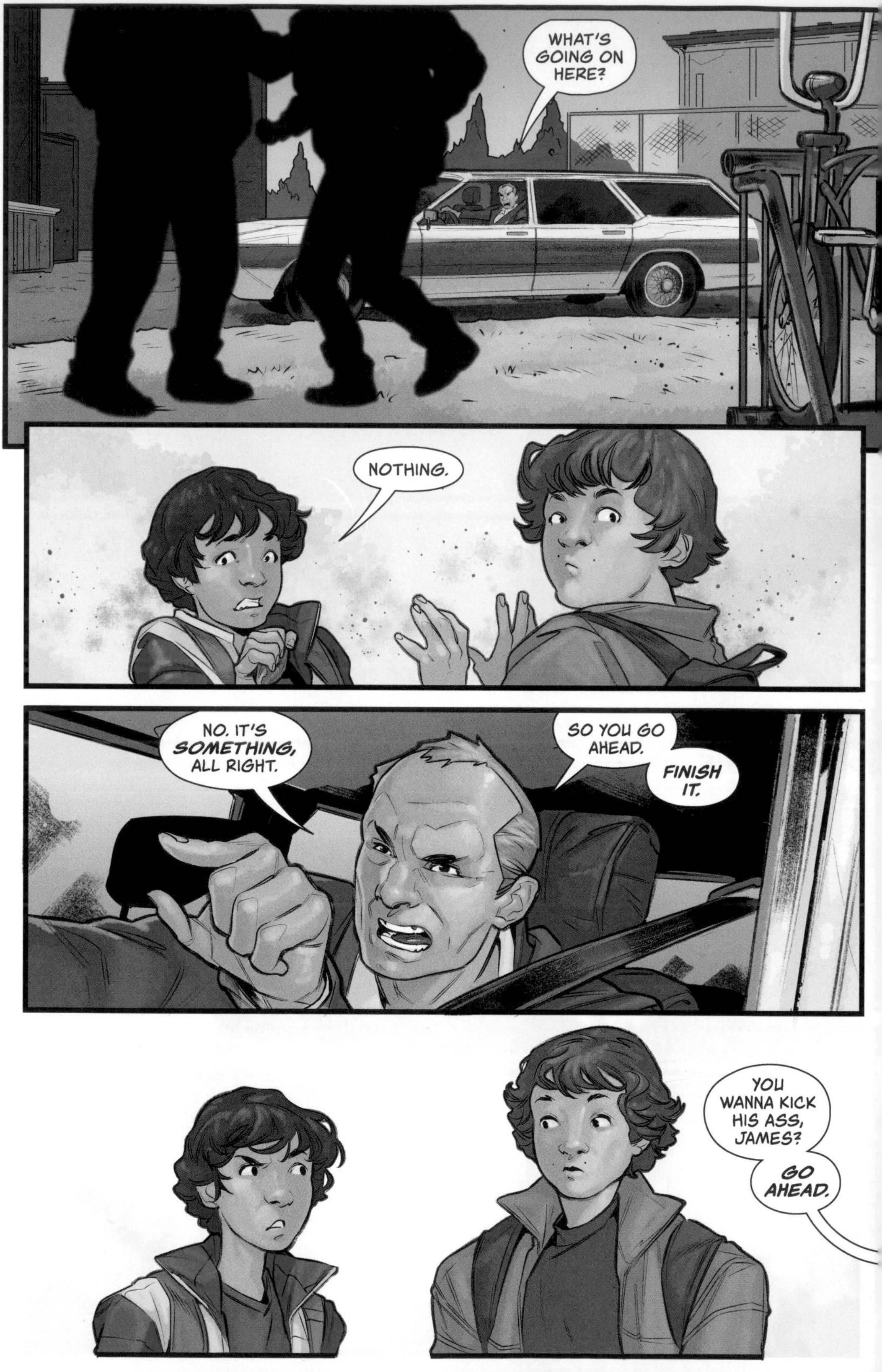
WHAT'S GOING ON HERE?
NOTHING.
NO. IT'S SOMETHING, ALL RIGHT.
SO YOU GO AHEAD.
FINISH IT.
YOU WANNA KICK HIS ASS, JAMES?
GO AHEAD.

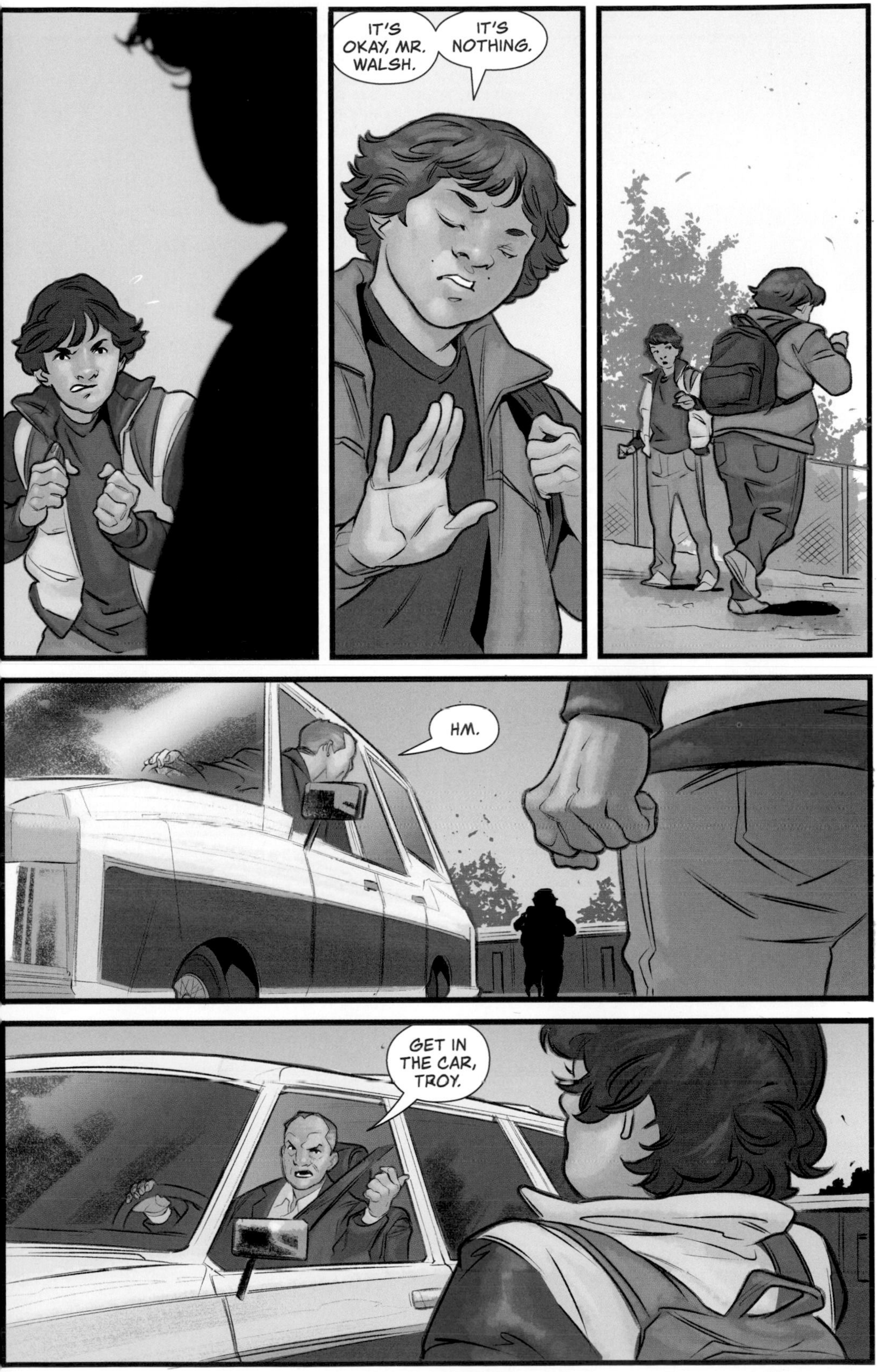
IT'S OKAY, MR. WALSH.
IT'S NOTHING.
HM.
GET IN THE CAR, TROY.

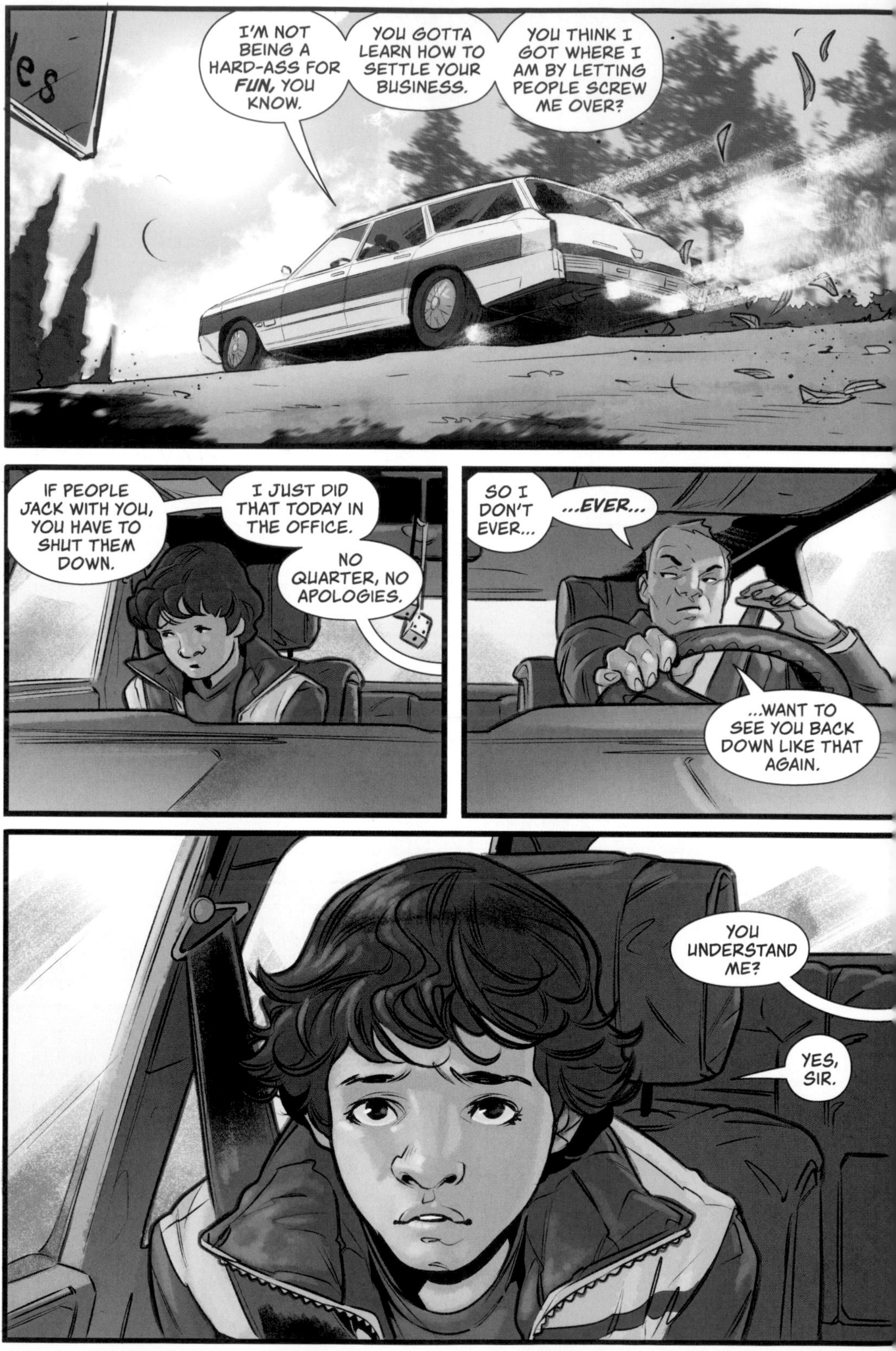

I'M NOT BEING A HARD-ASS FOR FUN, YOU KNOW.
YOU GOTTA LEARN HOW TO SETTLE YOUR BUSINESS.
YOU THINK I GOT WHERE I AM BY LETTING PEOPLE SCREW ME OVER?
IF PEOPLE JACK WITH YOU, YOU HAVE TO SHUT THEM DOWN.
I JUST DID THAT TODAY IN THE OFFICE.
NO QUARTER, NO APOLOGIES.
SO I DON'T EVER...
...EVER...
...WANT TO SEE YOU BACK DOWN LIKE THAT AGAIN.
YOU UNDERSTAND ME?
YES, SIR.

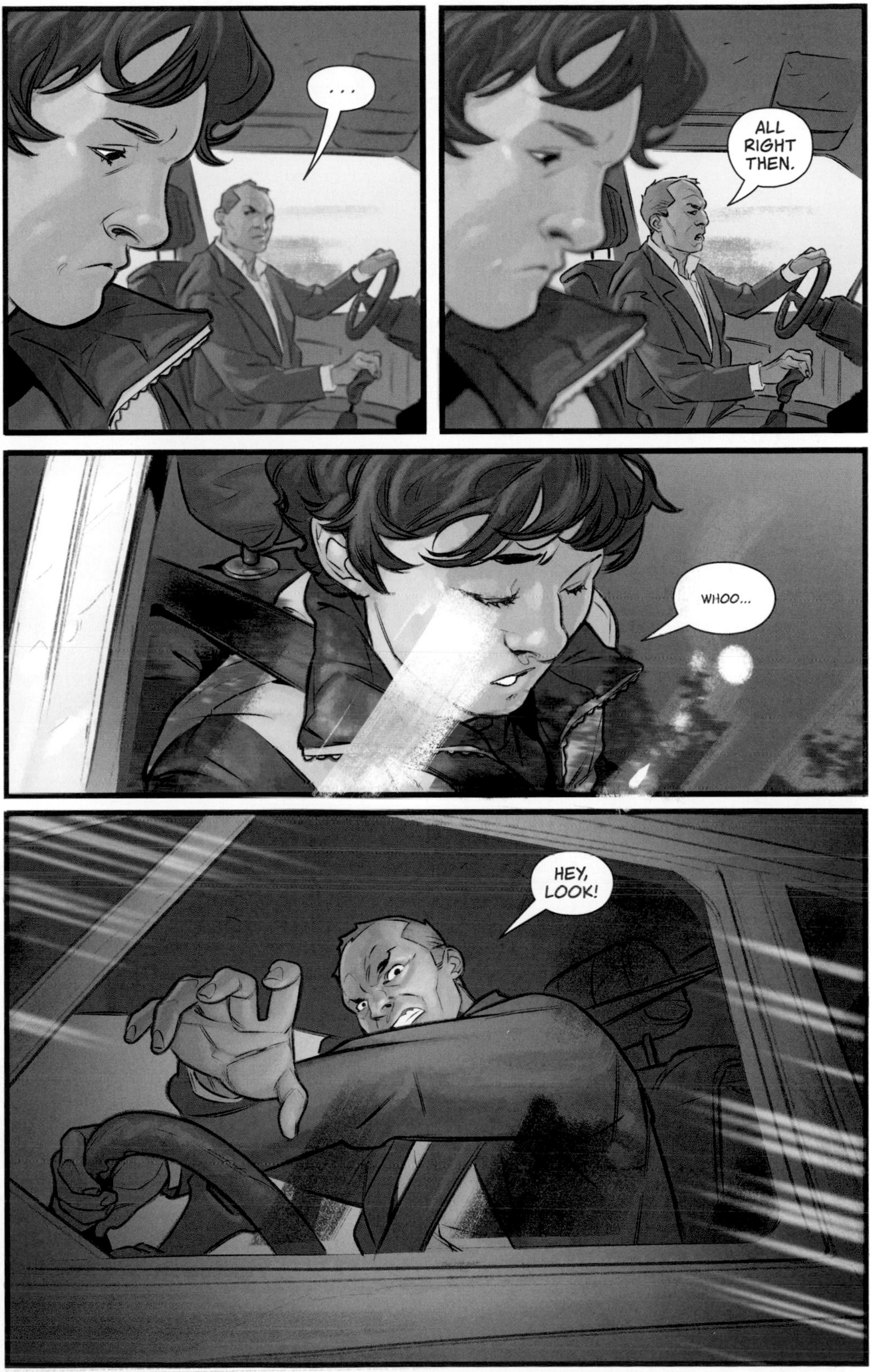
...
ALL RIGHT THEN.
WHOO...
HEY, LOOK!

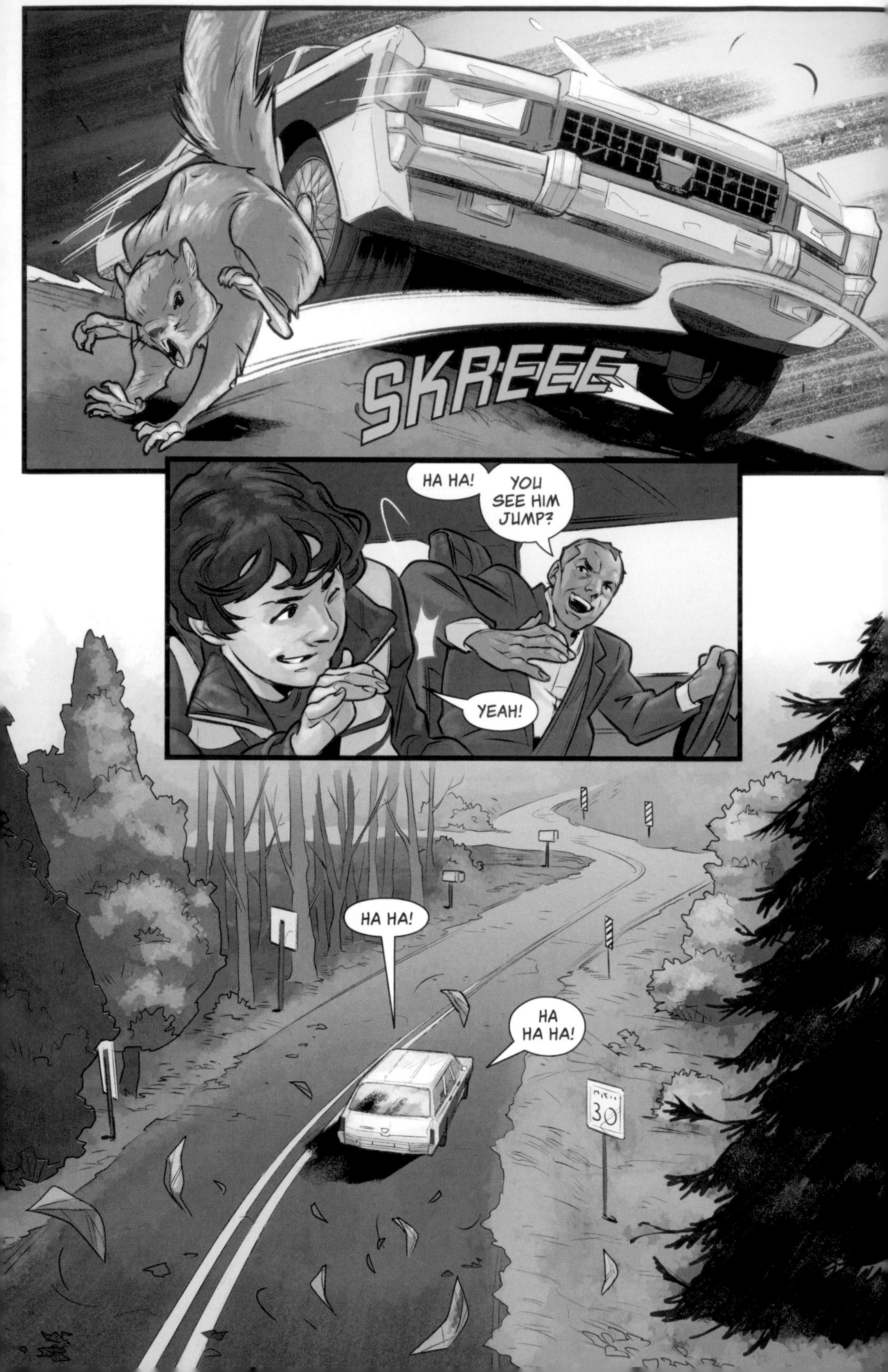
SKREEE
HA HA!
YOU SEE HIM JUMP?
YEAH!
HA HA!
HA HA HA!
30

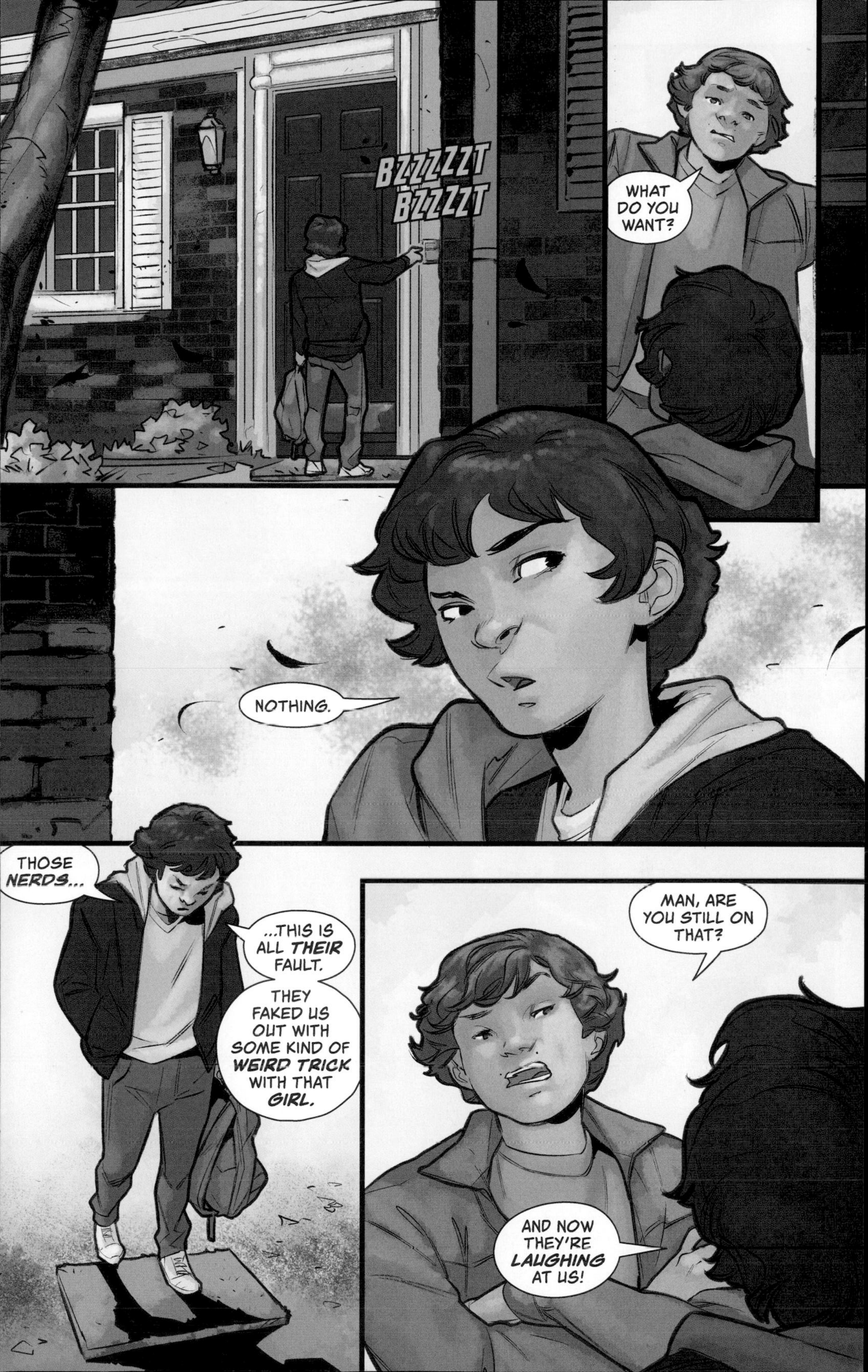
BZZZZZT
BZZZZT
WHAT DO YOU WANT?
NOTHING.
THOSE NERDS...
...THIS IS ALL THEIR FAULT.
THEY FAKED US OUT WITH SOME KIND OF WEIRD TRICK WITH THAT GIRL.
MAN, ARE YOU STILL ON THAT?
AND NOW THEY'RE LAUGHING AT US!

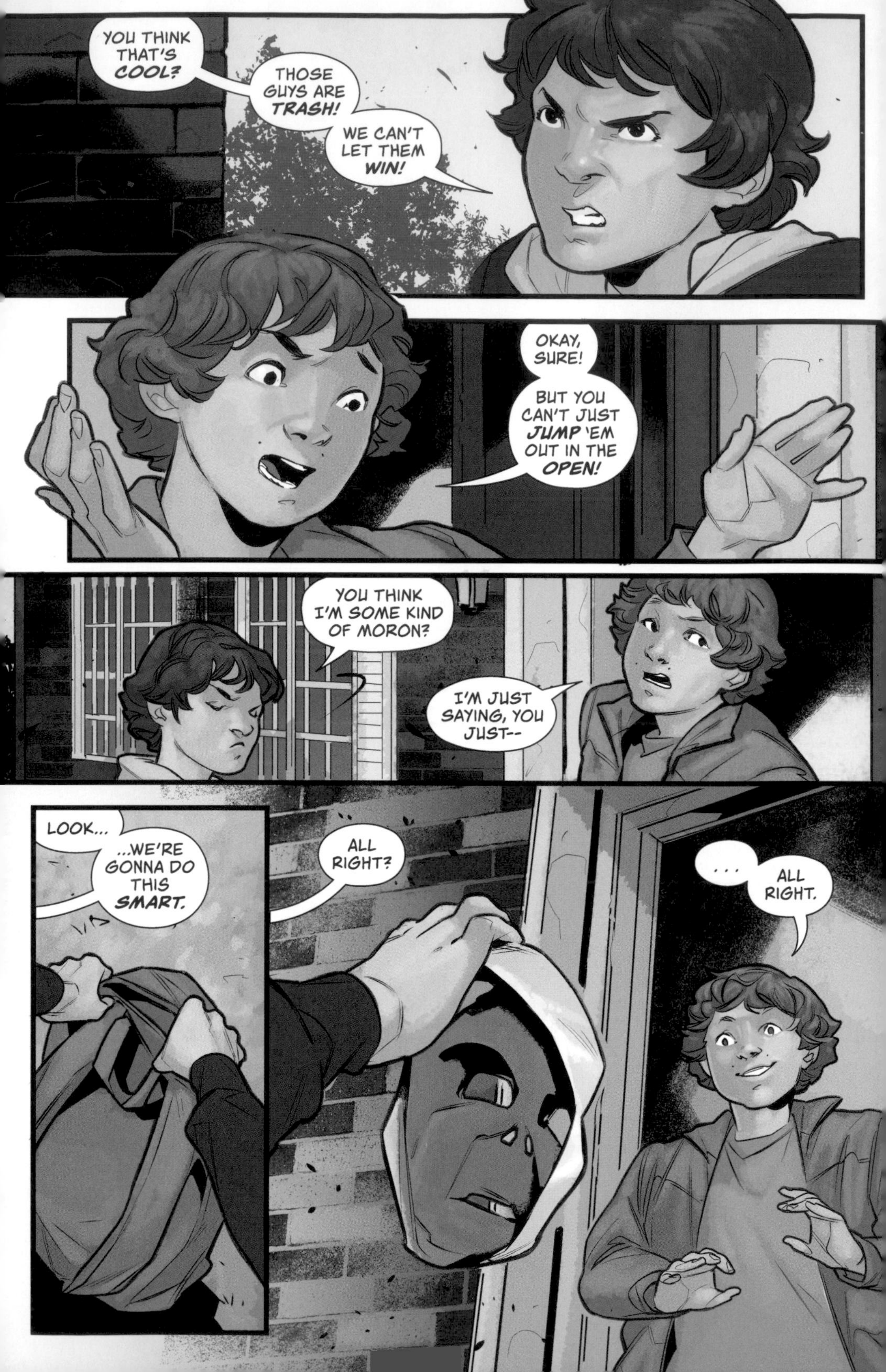
YOU THINK THAT'S COOL?
THOSE GUYS ARE TRASH!
WE CAN'T LET THEM WIN!
OKAY, SURE!
BUT YOU CAN'T JUST JUMP 'EM OUT IN THE OPEN!
YOU THINK I'M SOME KIND OF MORON?
I'M JUST SAYING, YOU JUST--
LOOK...
...WE'RE GONNA DO THIS SMART.
ALL RIGHT?
. . .
ALL RIGHT.

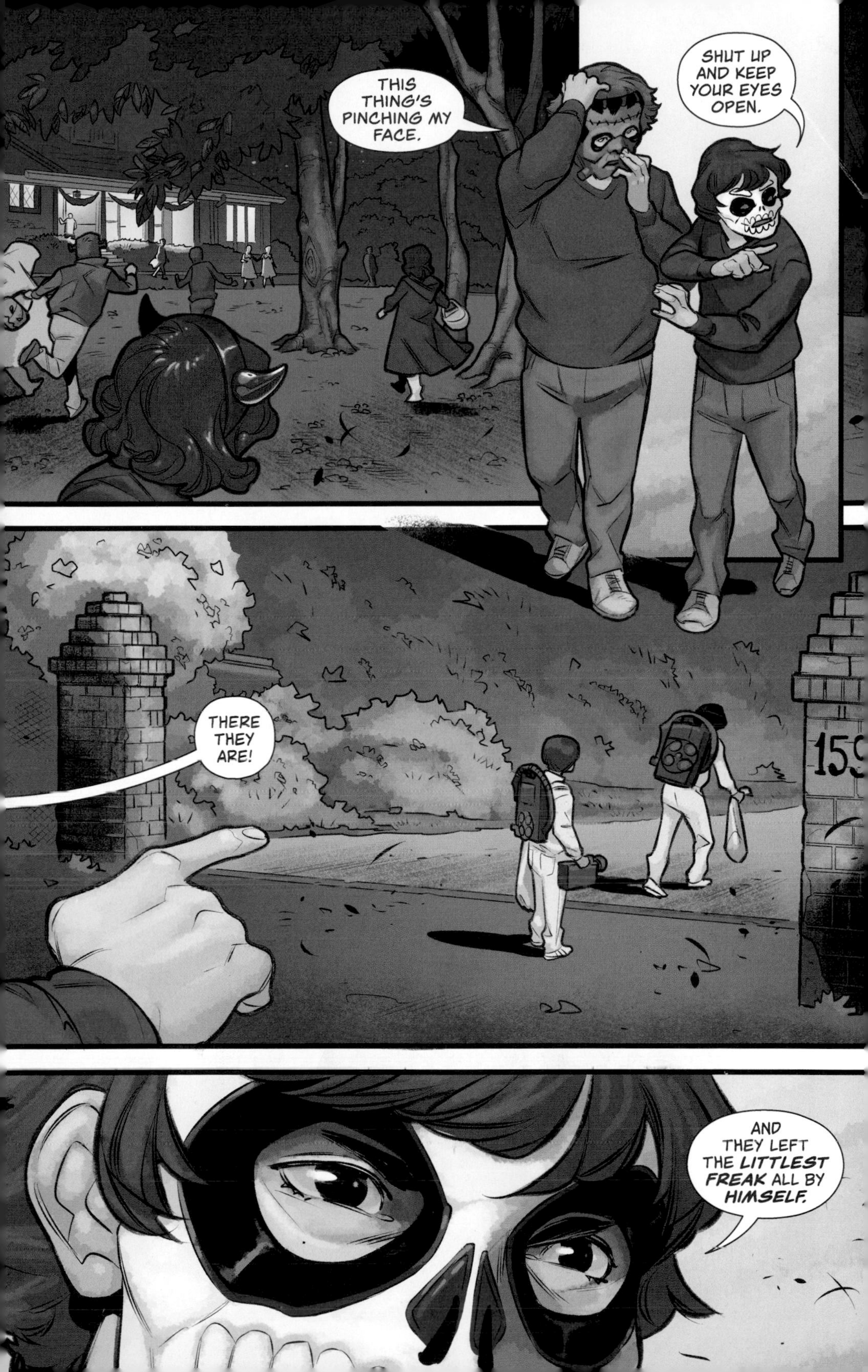
THIS THING'S PINCHING MY FACE.
SHUT UP AND KEEP YOUR EYES OPEN.
THERE THEY ARE!
159
AND THEY LEFT THE *LITTLEST FREAK* ALL BY *HIMSELF.*

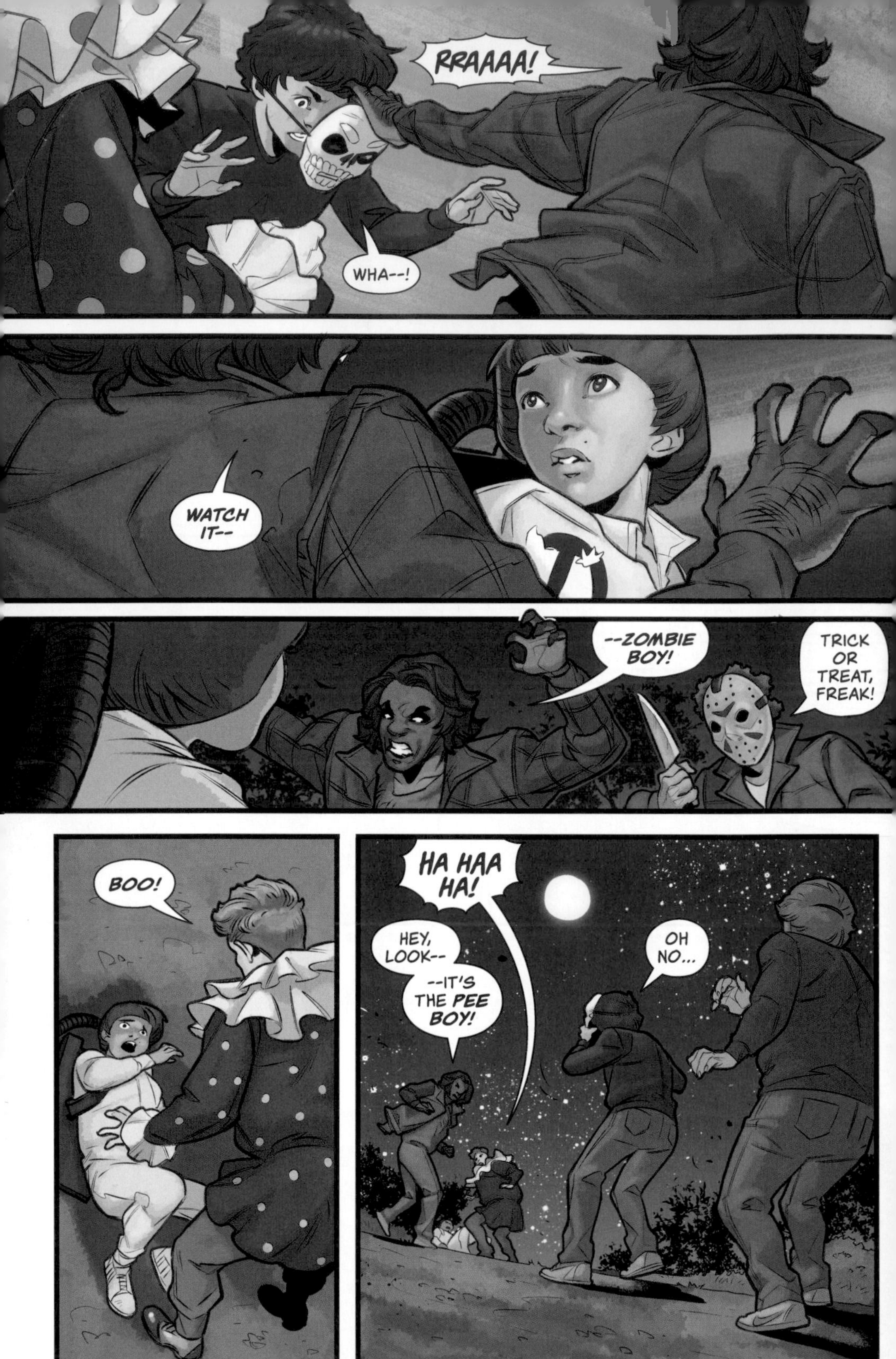
RRAAAA!
WHA--!
WATCH IT--
--ZOMBIE BOY!
TRICK OR TREAT, FREAK!
BOO!
HA HAA HA!
HEY, LOOK--
--IT'S THE PEE BOY!
OH NO...

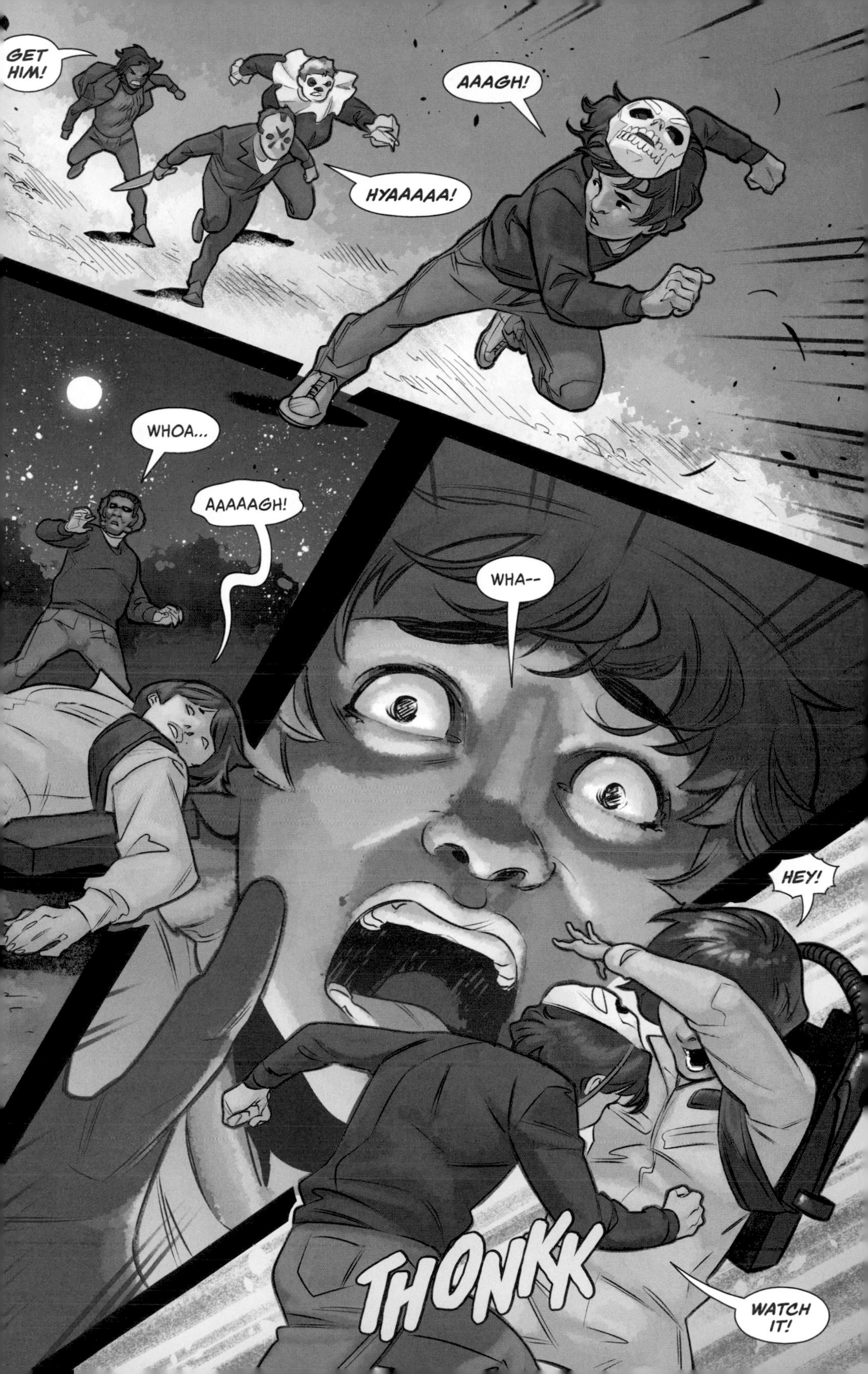
GET HIM!
AAAGH!
HYAAAAA!
WHOA...
AAAAAGH!
WHA--
HEY!
THONKK
WATCH IT!

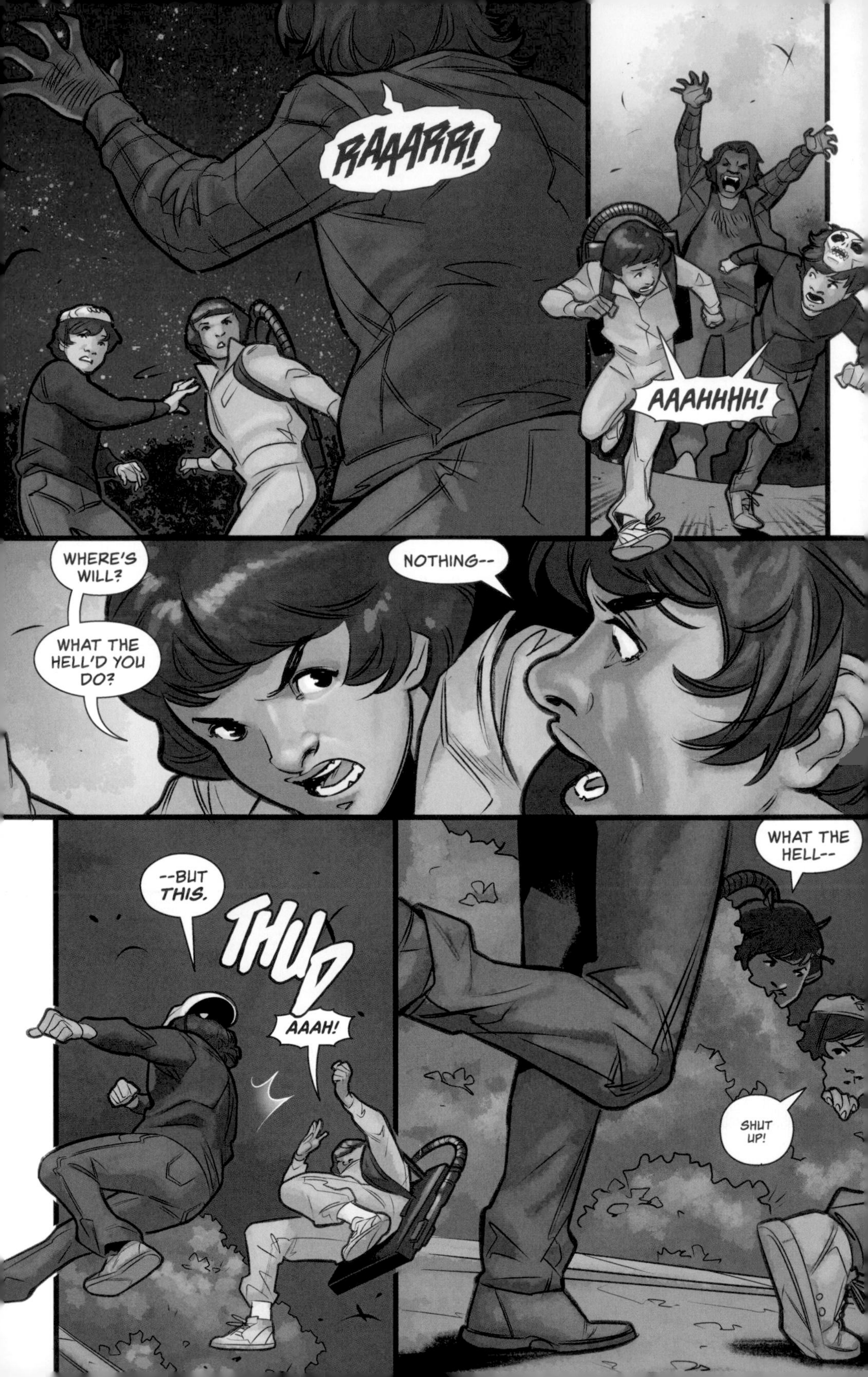
RAAARR!
AAAHHHH!
WHERE'S WILL?
WHAT THE HELL'D YOU DO?
NOTHING--
--BUT THIS.
THUD
AAAH!
WHAT THE HELL--
SHUT UP!

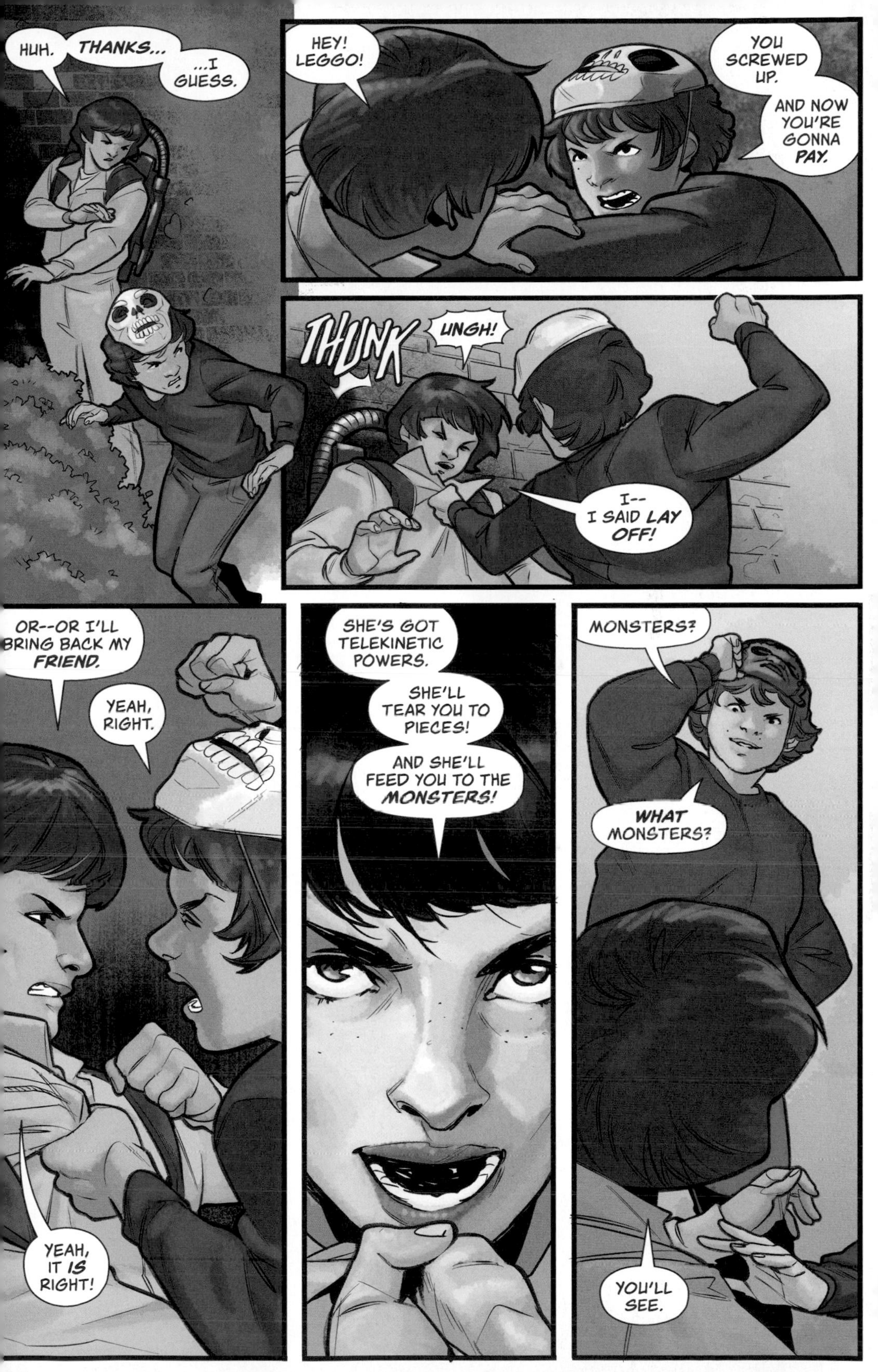
HUH.
THANKS...
...I GUESS.
HEY! LEGGO!
YOU SCREWED UP.
AND NOW YOU'RE GONNA PAY.
THUNK
UNGH!
I-- I SAID LAY OFF!
OR--OR I'LL BRING BACK MY FRIEND.
YEAH, RIGHT.
YEAH, IT IS RIGHT!
SHE'S GOT TELEKINETIC POWERS.
SHE'LL TEAR YOU TO PIECES!
AND SHE'LL FEED YOU TO THE MONSTERS!
MONSTERS?
WHAT MONSTERS?
YOU'LL SEE.

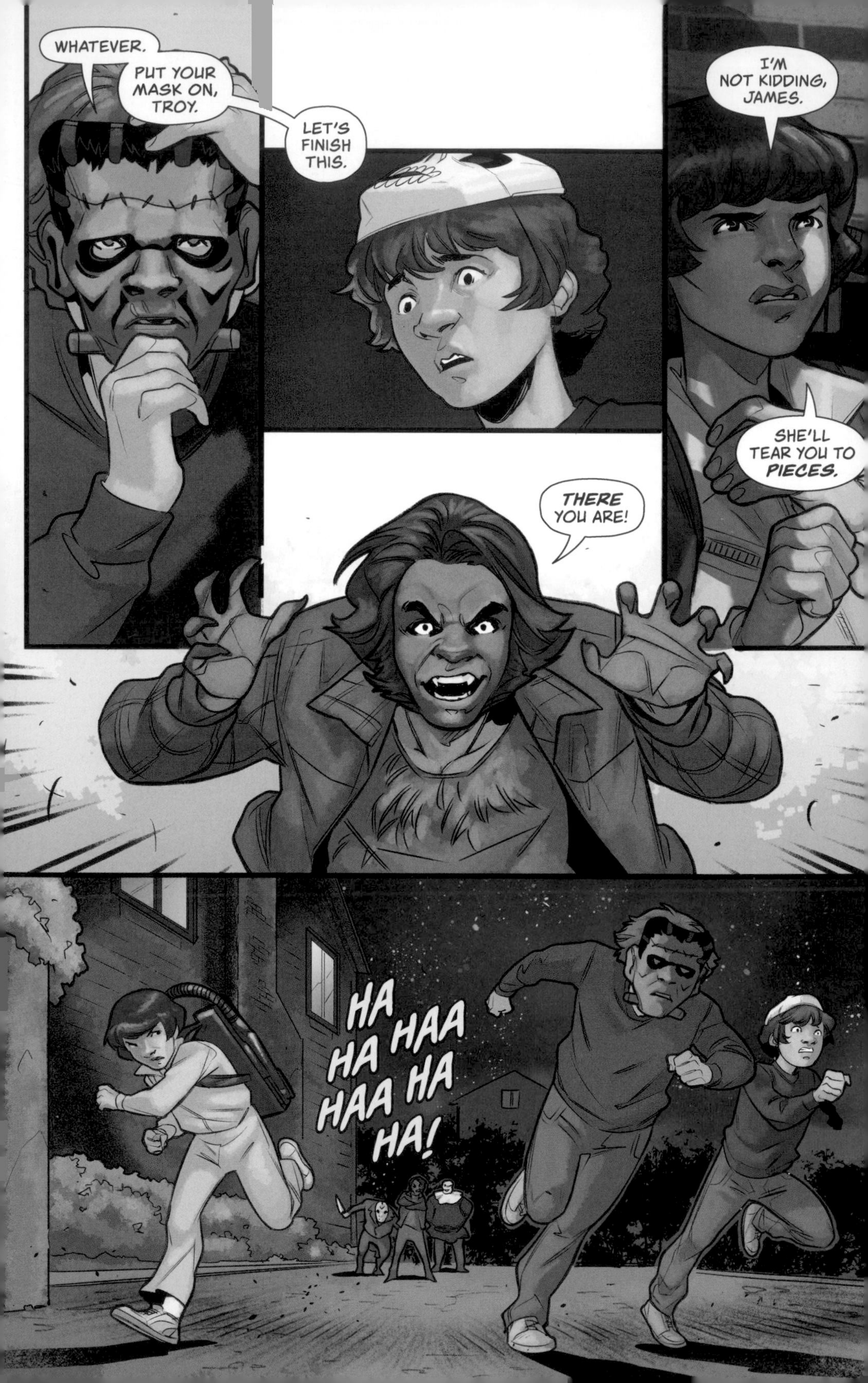
WHATEVER.
PUT YOUR MASK ON, TROY.
LET'S FINISH THIS.
I'M NOT KIDDING, JAMES.
SHE'LL TEAR YOU TO PIECES.
THERE YOU ARE!
HA HA HAA HA HAA HA HA!

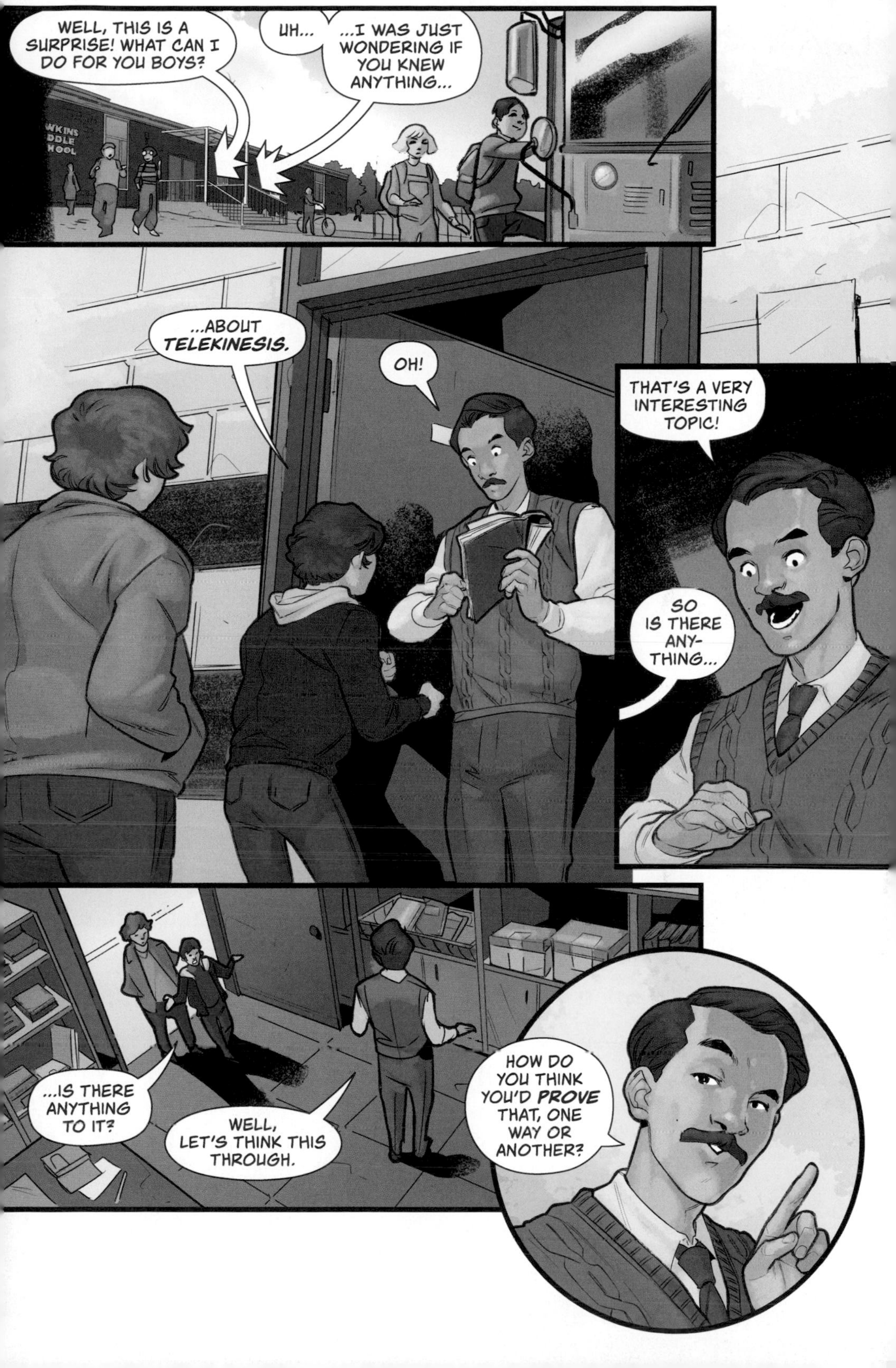

WELL, THIS IS A SURPRISE! WHAT CAN I DO FOR YOU BOYS?
UH...
...I WAS JUST WONDERING IF YOU KNEW ANYTHING...
...ABOUT *TELEKINESIS.*
OH!
THAT'S A VERY INTERESTING TOPIC!
SO IS THERE ANY-THING...
...IS THERE ANYTHING TO IT?
WELL, LET'S THINK THIS THROUGH.
HOW DO YOU THINK YOU'D *PROVE* THAT, ONE WAY OR ANOTHER?

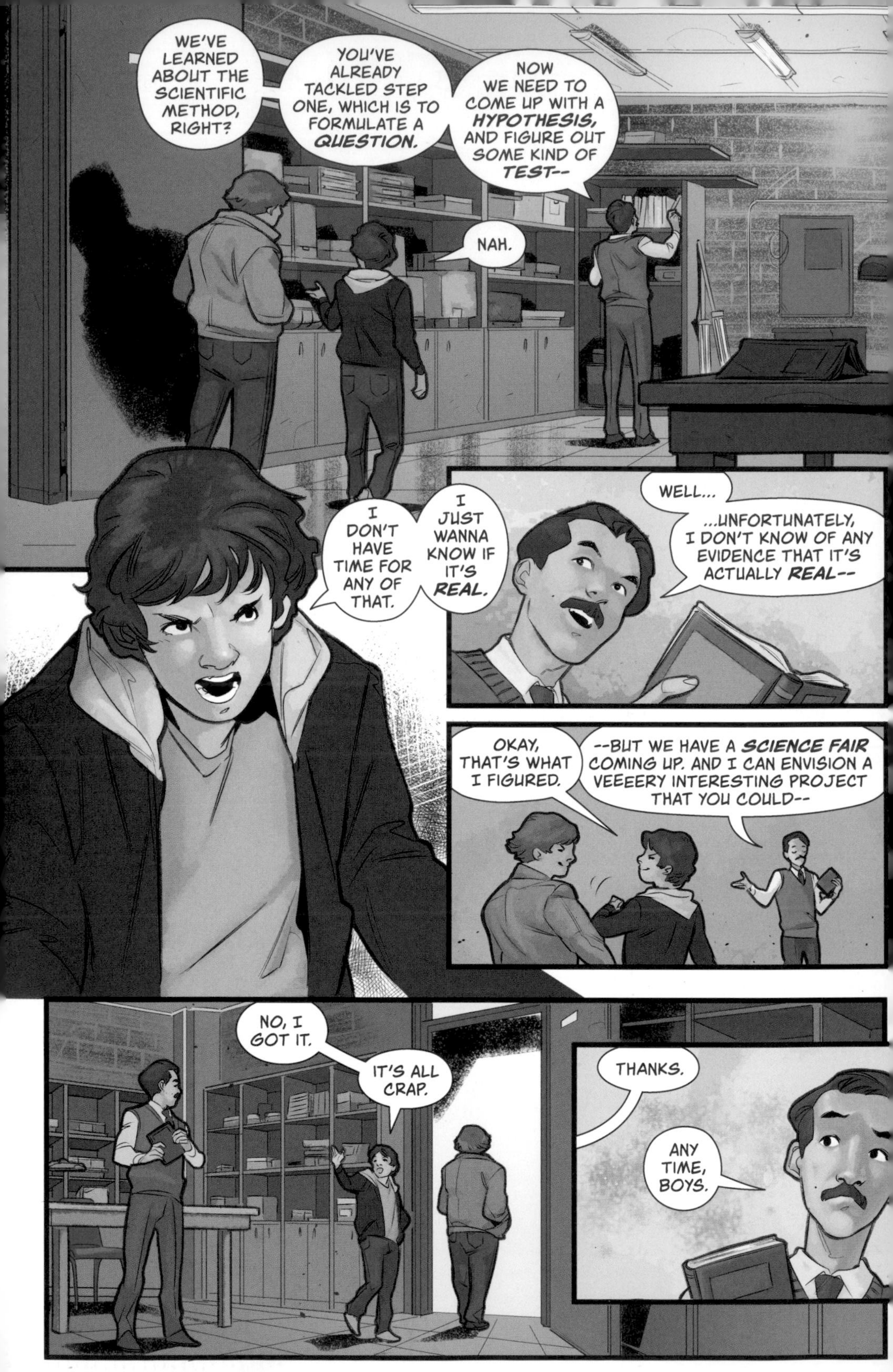
WE'VE LEARNED ABOUT THE SCIENTIFIC METHOD, RIGHT?
YOU'VE ALREADY TACKLED STEP ONE, WHICH IS TO FORMULATE A *QUESTION.*
NOW WE NEED TO COME UP WITH A *HYPOTHESIS,* AND FIGURE OUT SOME KIND OF *TEST--*
NAH.
I DON'T HAVE TIME FOR ANY OF THAT.
I JUST WANNA KNOW IF IT'S *REAL.*
WELL...
...UNFORTUNATELY, I DON'T KNOW OF ANY EVIDENCE THAT IT'S ACTUALLY *REAL--*
OKAY, THAT'S WHAT I FIGURED.
--BUT WE HAVE A *SCIENCE FAIR* COMING UP. AND I CAN ENVISION A VEEEERY INTERESTING PROJECT THAT YOU COULD--
NO, I GOT IT.
IT'S ALL CRAP.
THANKS.
ANY TIME, BOYS.

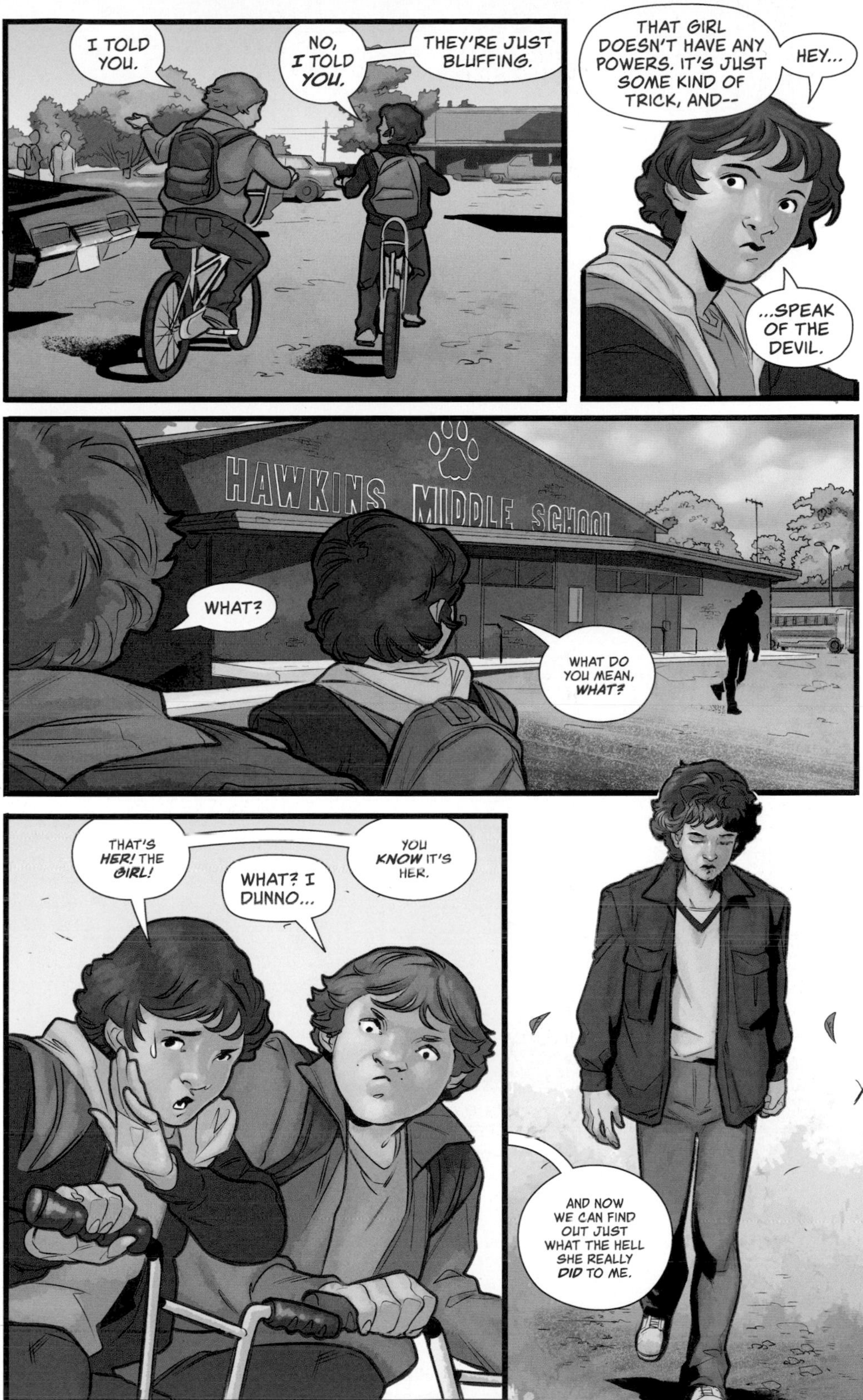
I TOLD YOU.
NO, I TOLD YOU.
THEY'RE JUST BLUFFING.
THAT GIRL DOESN'T HAVE ANY POWERS. IT'S JUST SOME KIND OF TRICK, AND--
HEY...
...SPEAK OF THE DEVIL.
HAWKINS MIDDLE SCHOOL
WHAT?
WHAT DO YOU MEAN, WHAT?
THAT'S HER! THE GIRL!
WHAT? I DUNNO...
YOU KNOW IT'S HER.
AND NOW WE CAN FIND OUT JUST WHAT THE HELL SHE REALLY DID TO ME.

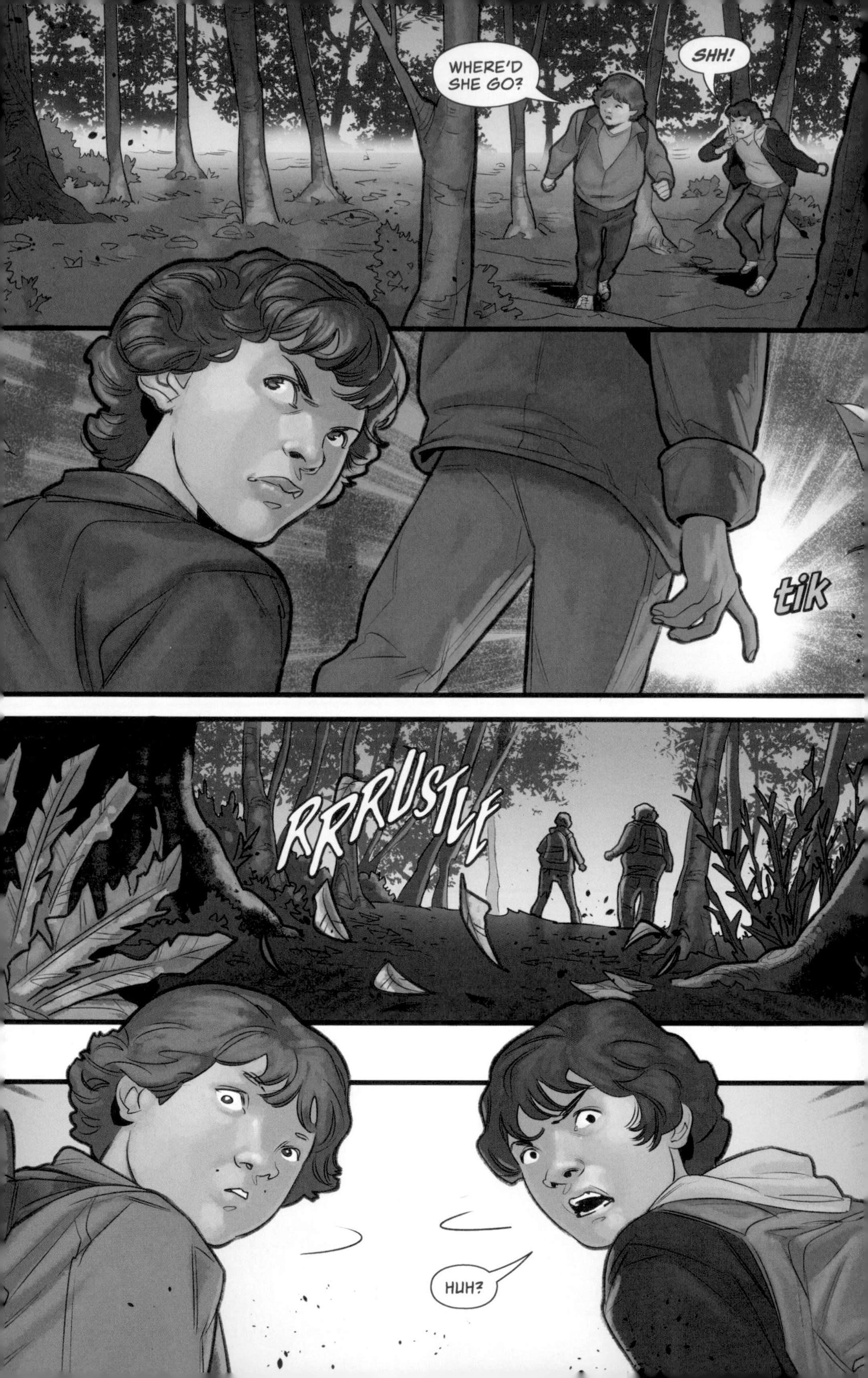
WHERE'D SHE GO?
SHH!
tik
RRRUSTLE
HUH?

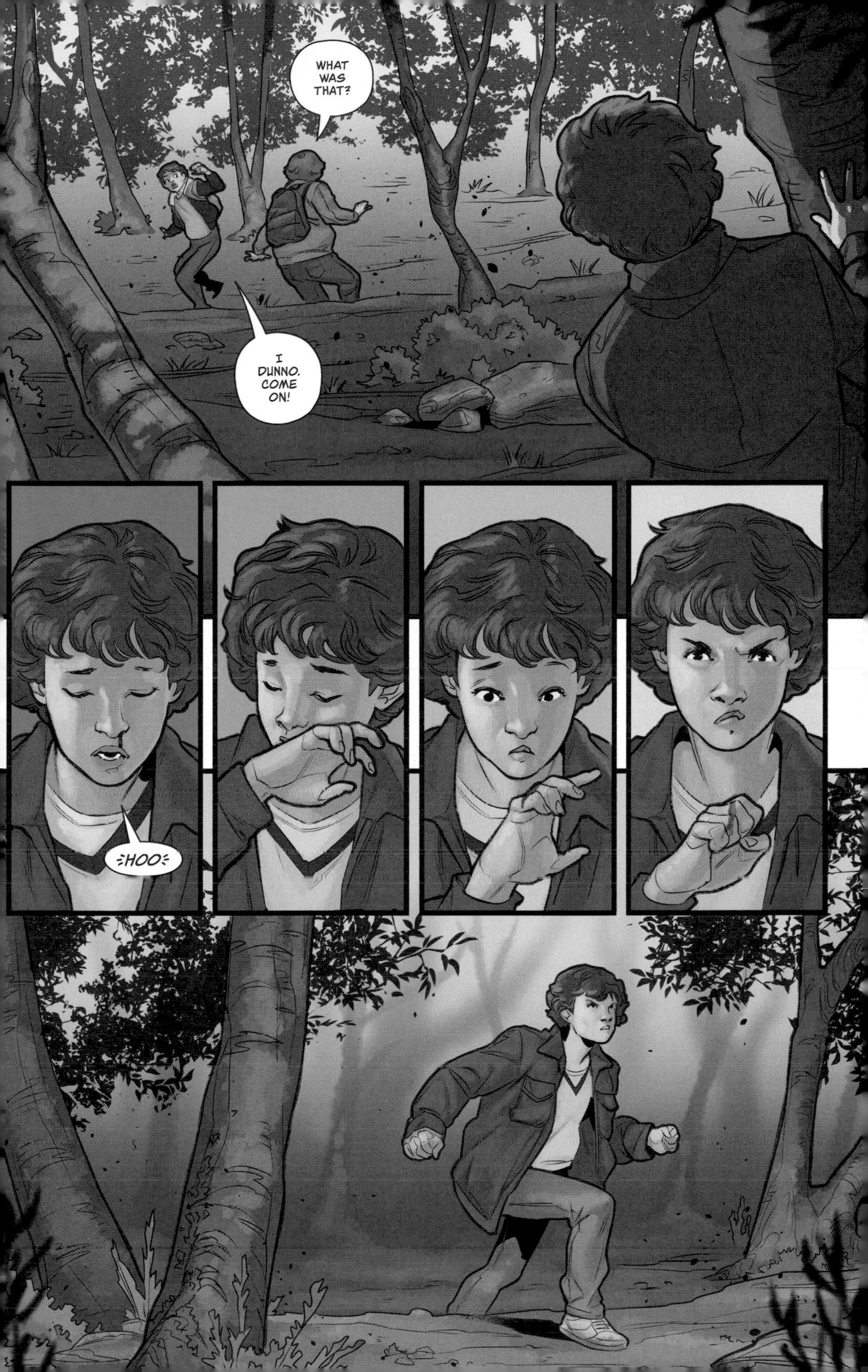
WHAT WAS THAT?
I DUNNO. COME ON!
HOO

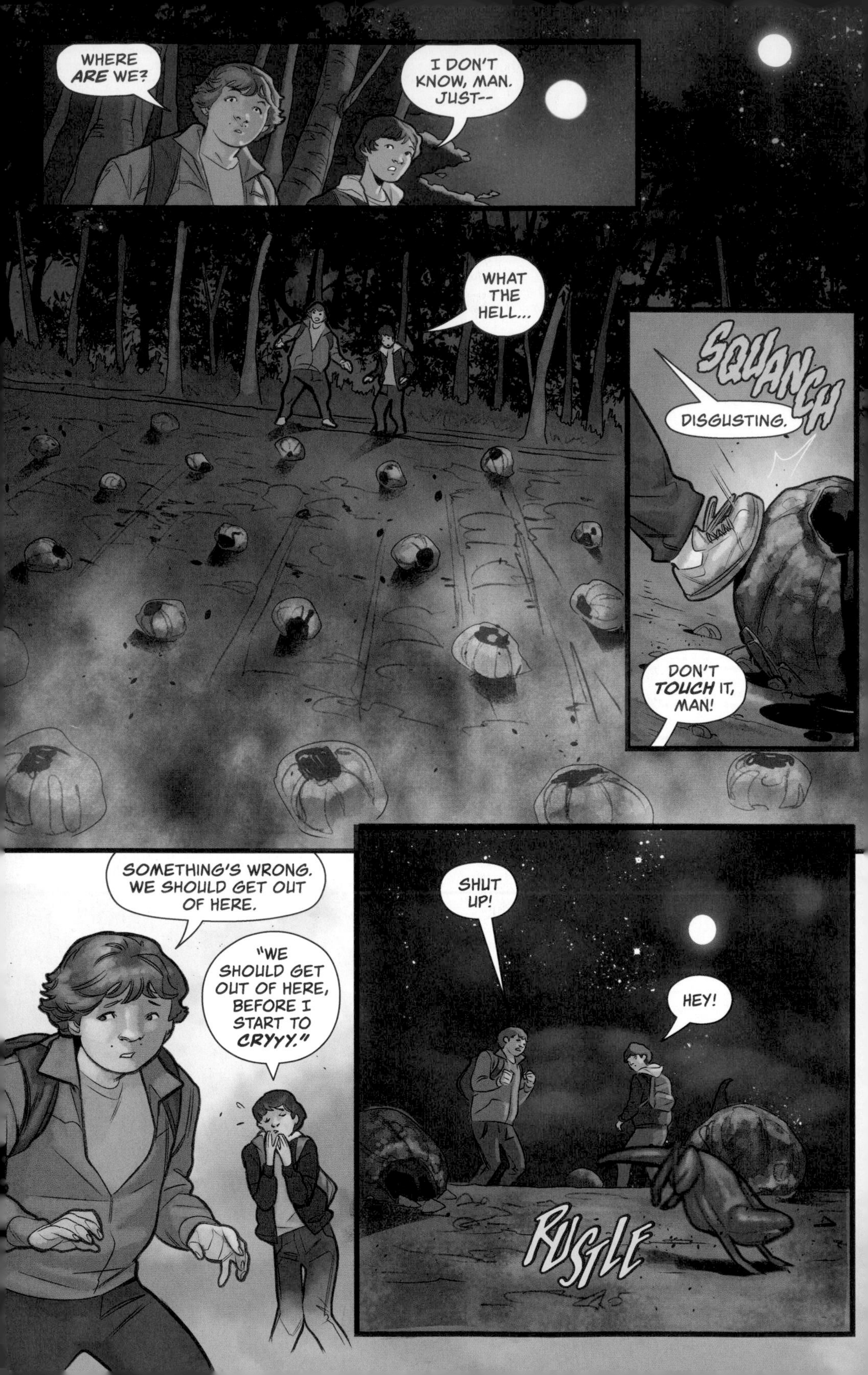
WHERE ARE WE?
I DON'T KNOW, MAN. JUST--
WHAT THE HELL...
SQUANCH
DISGUSTING.
DON'T TOUCH IT, MAN!
SOMETHING'S WRONG. WE SHOULD GET OUT OF HERE.
"WE SHOULD GET OUT OF HERE, BEFORE I START TO CRYYY."
SHUT UP!
HEY!
RUSTLE

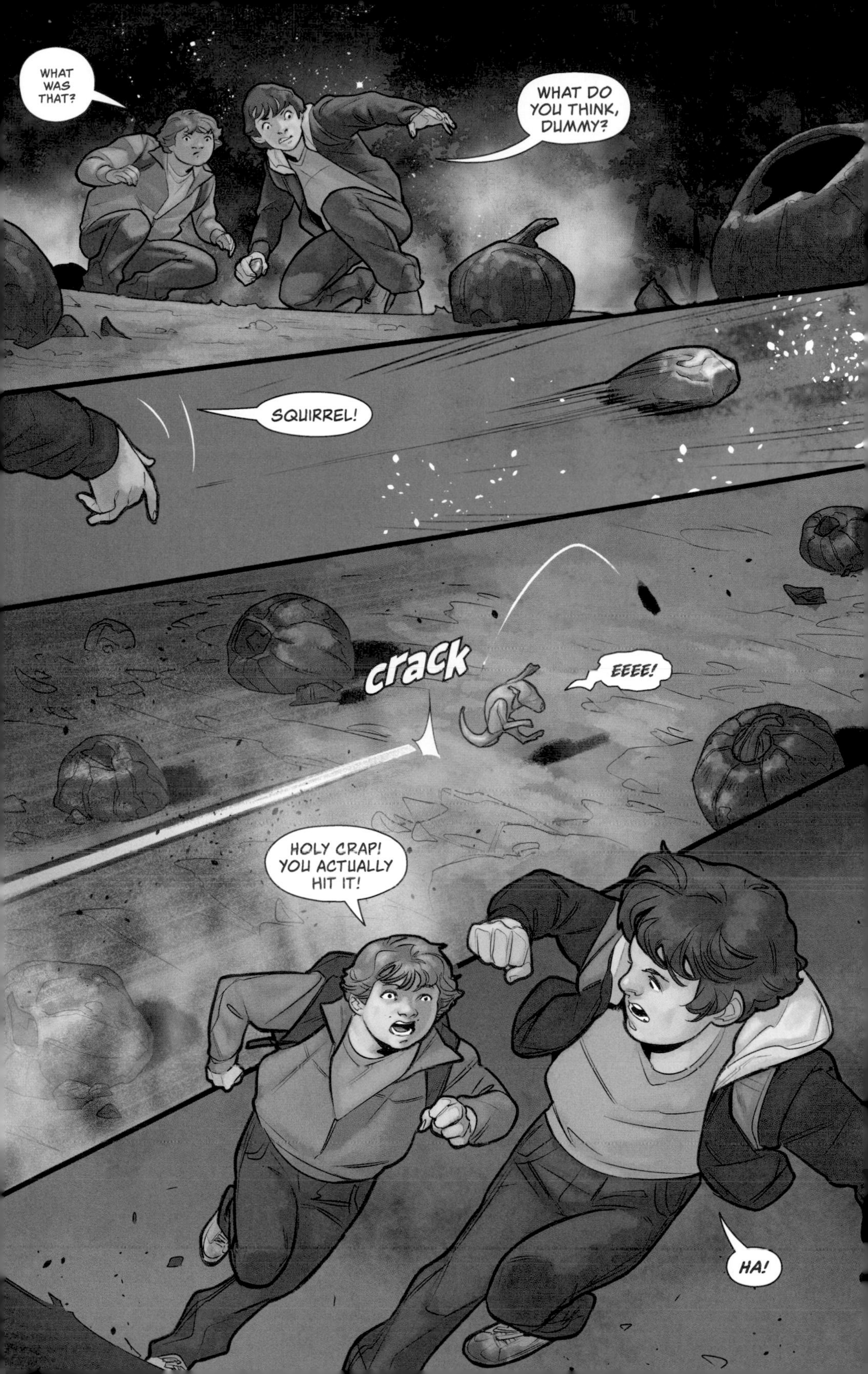
WHAT WAS THAT?
WHAT DO YOU THINK, DUMMY?
SQUIRREL!
crack
EEEE!
HOLY CRAP! YOU ACTUALLY HIT IT!
HA!

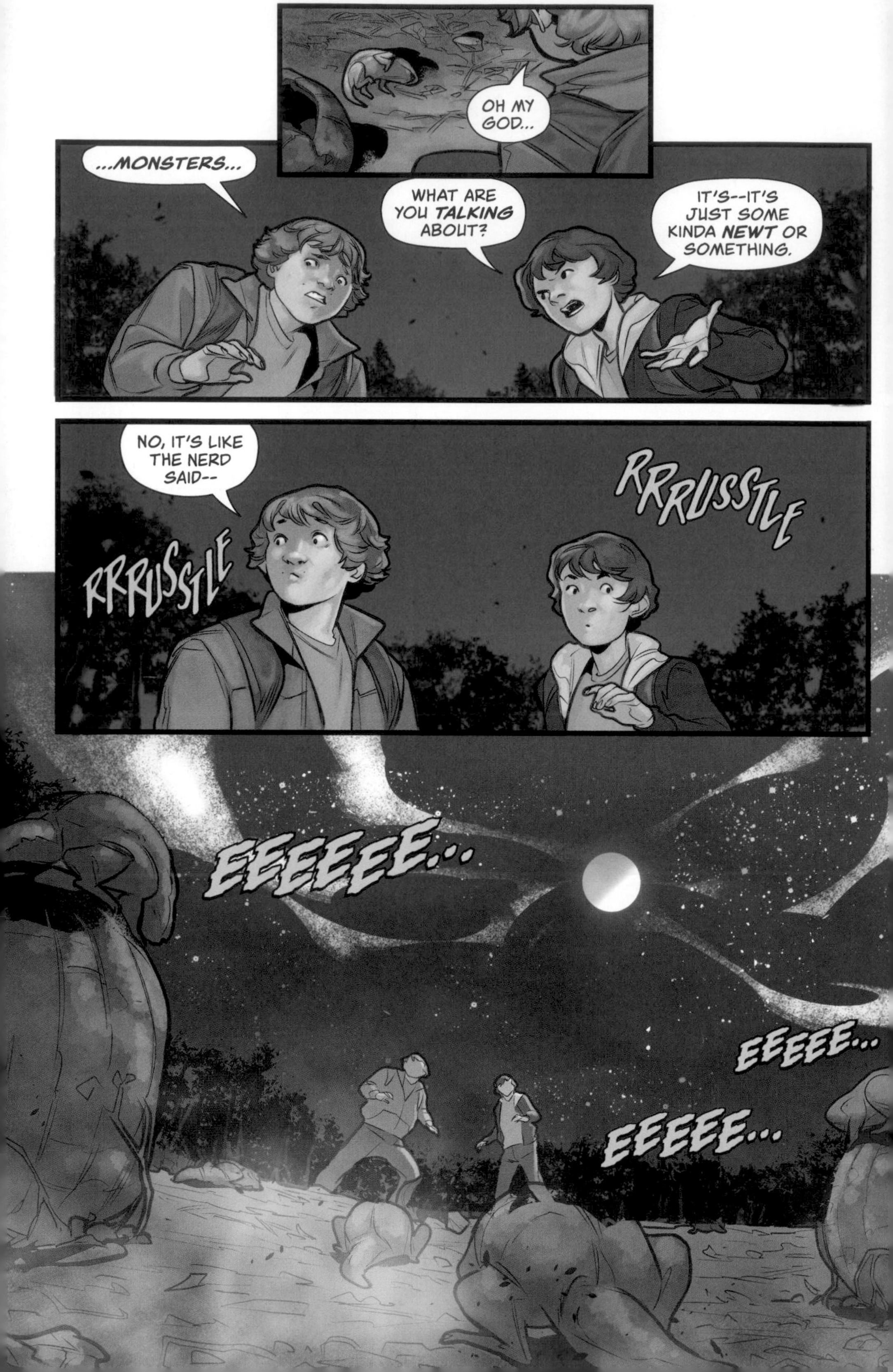
OH MY GOD...
...MONSTERS...
WHAT ARE YOU TALKING ABOUT?
IT'S--IT'S JUST SOME KINDA NEWT OR SOMETHING.
NO, IT'S LIKE THE NERD SAID--
RRRUSSTLE
RRRUSSTLE
EEEEEE...
EEEEE...
EEEEE...

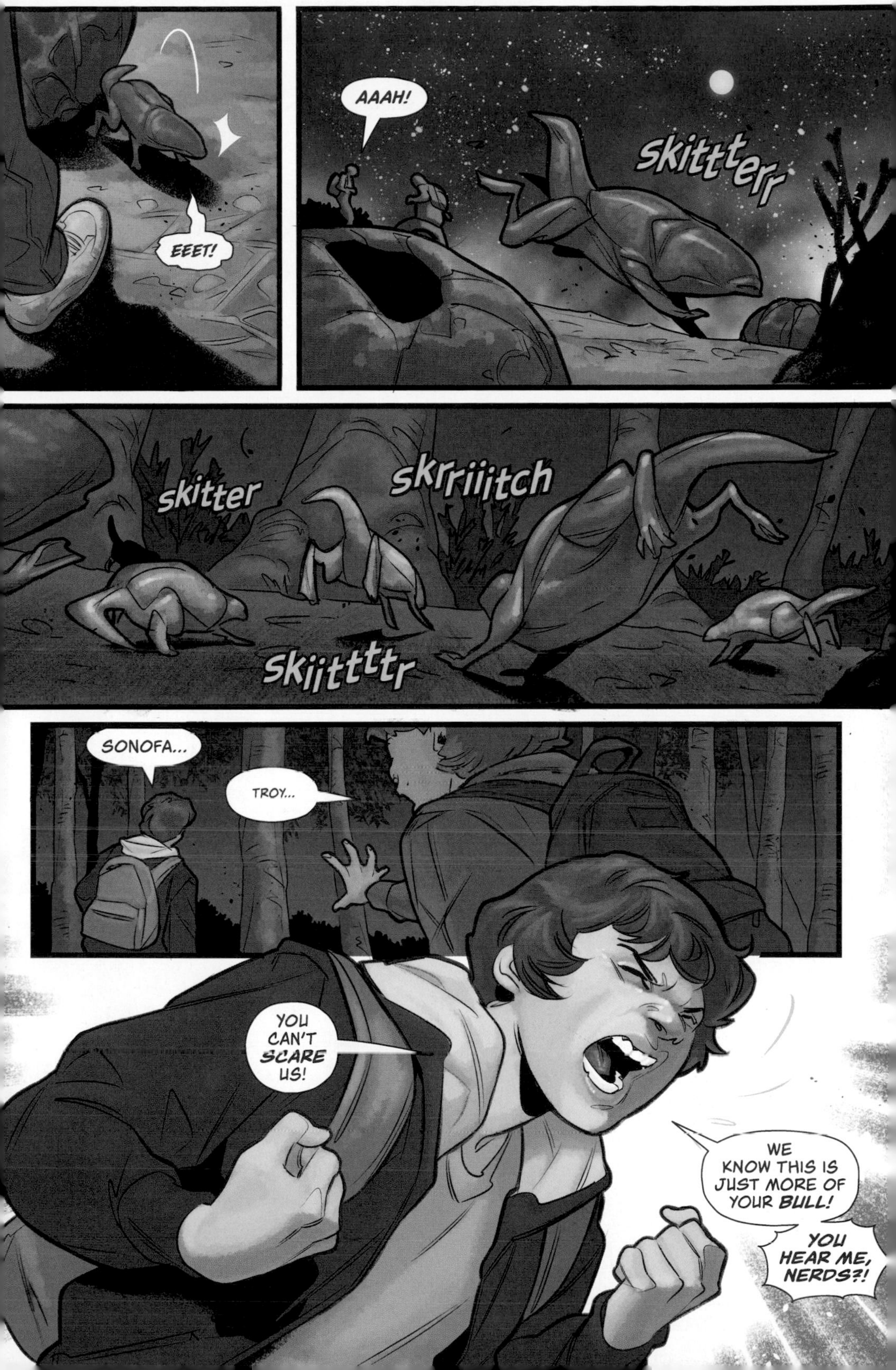
EEET!
AAAH!
Skittterr
skitter
skrriiiitch
Skiittttr
SONOFA...
TROY...
YOU CAN'T SCARE US!
WE KNOW THIS IS JUST MORE OF YOUR BULL!
YOU HEAR ME, NERDS?!

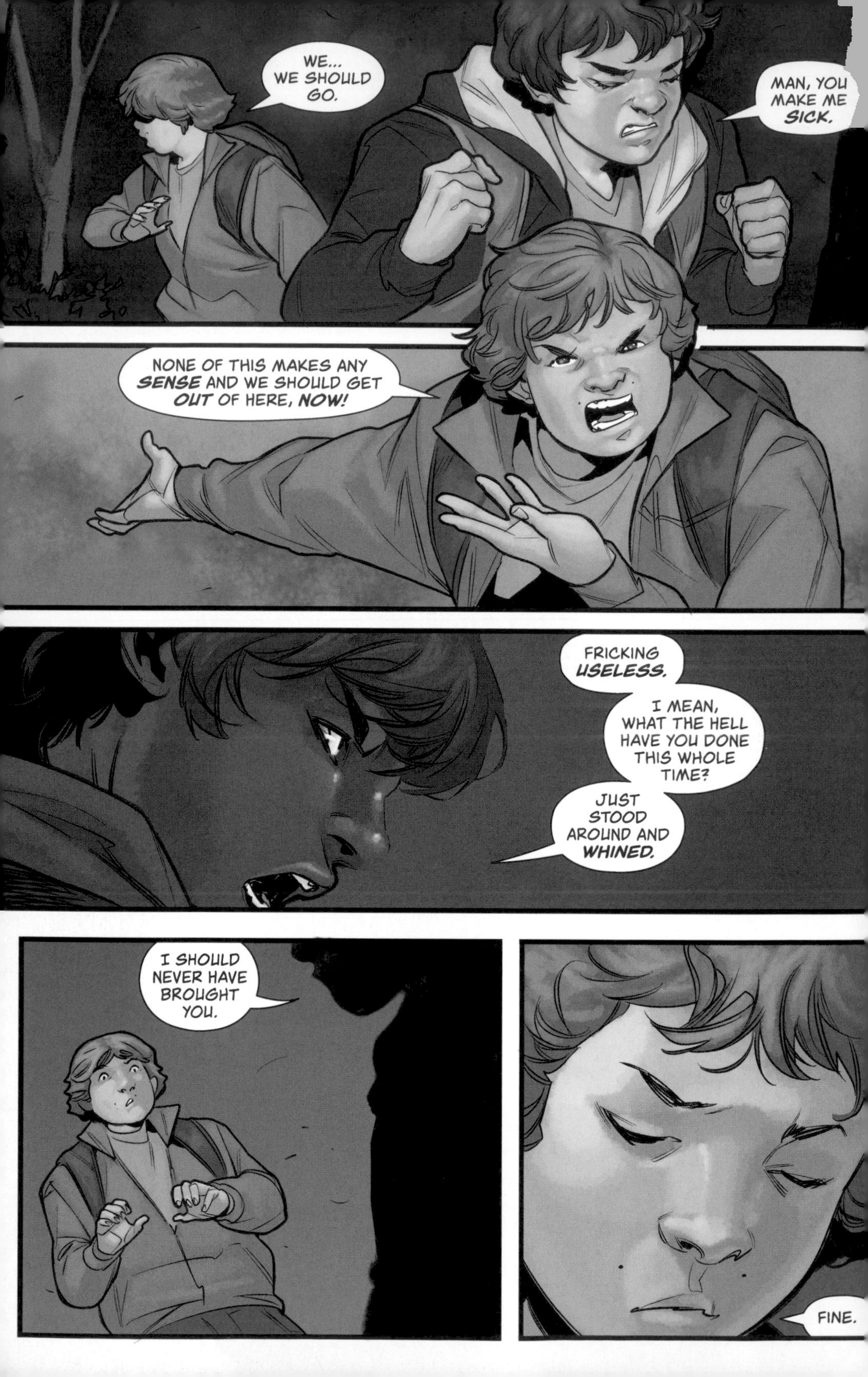
WE... WE SHOULD GO.
MAN, YOU MAKE ME SICK.
NONE OF THIS MAKES ANY SENSE AND WE SHOULD GET OUT OF HERE, NOW!
FRICKING USELESS.
I MEAN, WHAT THE HELL HAVE YOU DONE THIS WHOLE TIME?
JUST STOOD AROUND AND WHINED.
I SHOULD NEVER HAVE BROUGHT YOU.
FINE.

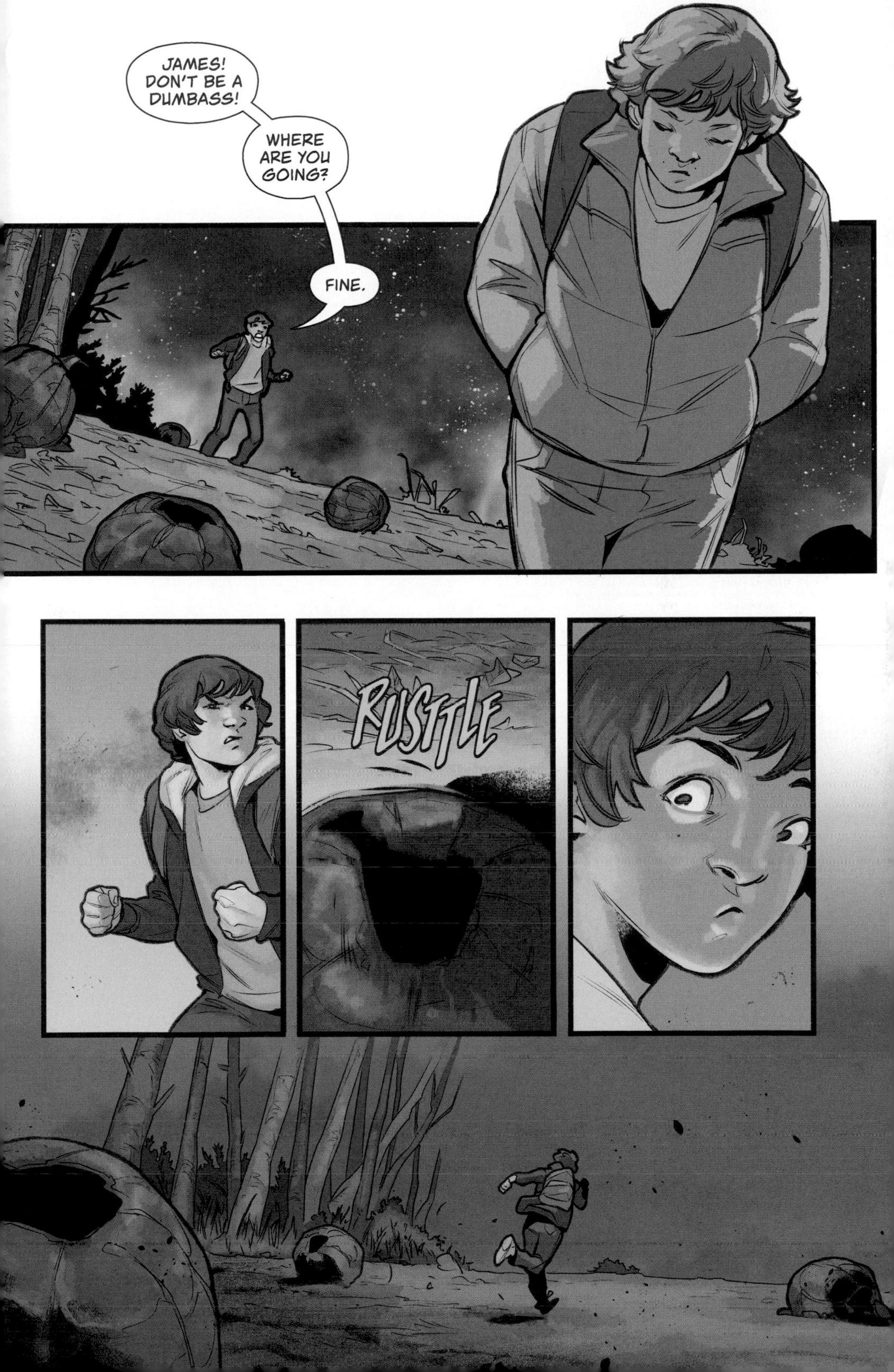
JAMES! DON'T BE A DUMBASS!
WHERE ARE YOU GOING?
FINE.
RUSTLE

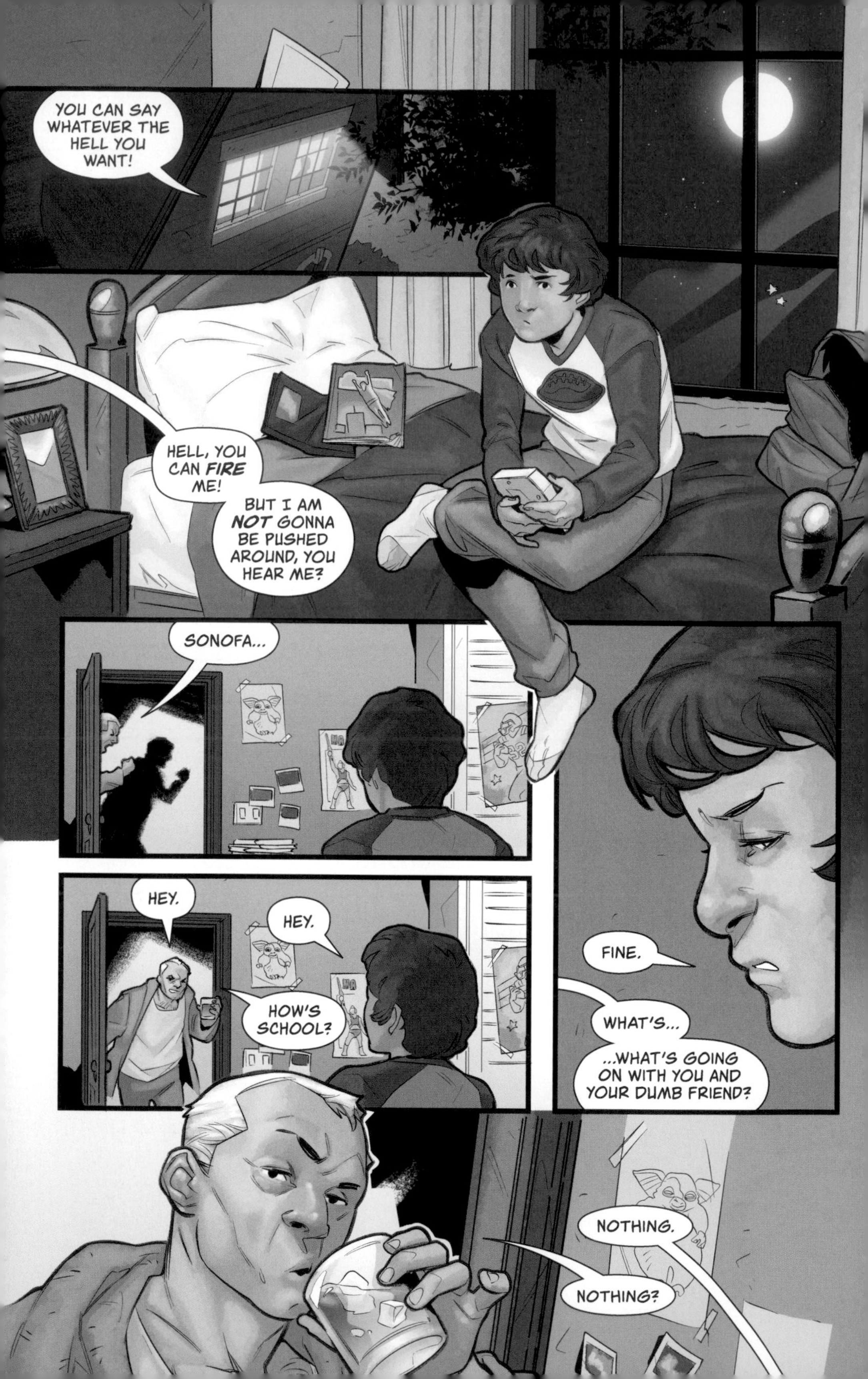
YOU CAN SAY WHATEVER THE HELL YOU WANT!
HELL, YOU CAN FIRE ME!
BUT I AM NOT GONNA BE PUSHED AROUND, YOU HEAR ME?
SONOFA...
HEY.
HEY.
HOW'S SCHOOL?
FINE.
WHAT'S...
...WHAT'S GOING ON WITH YOU AND YOUR DUMB FRIEND?
NOTHING.
NOTHING?

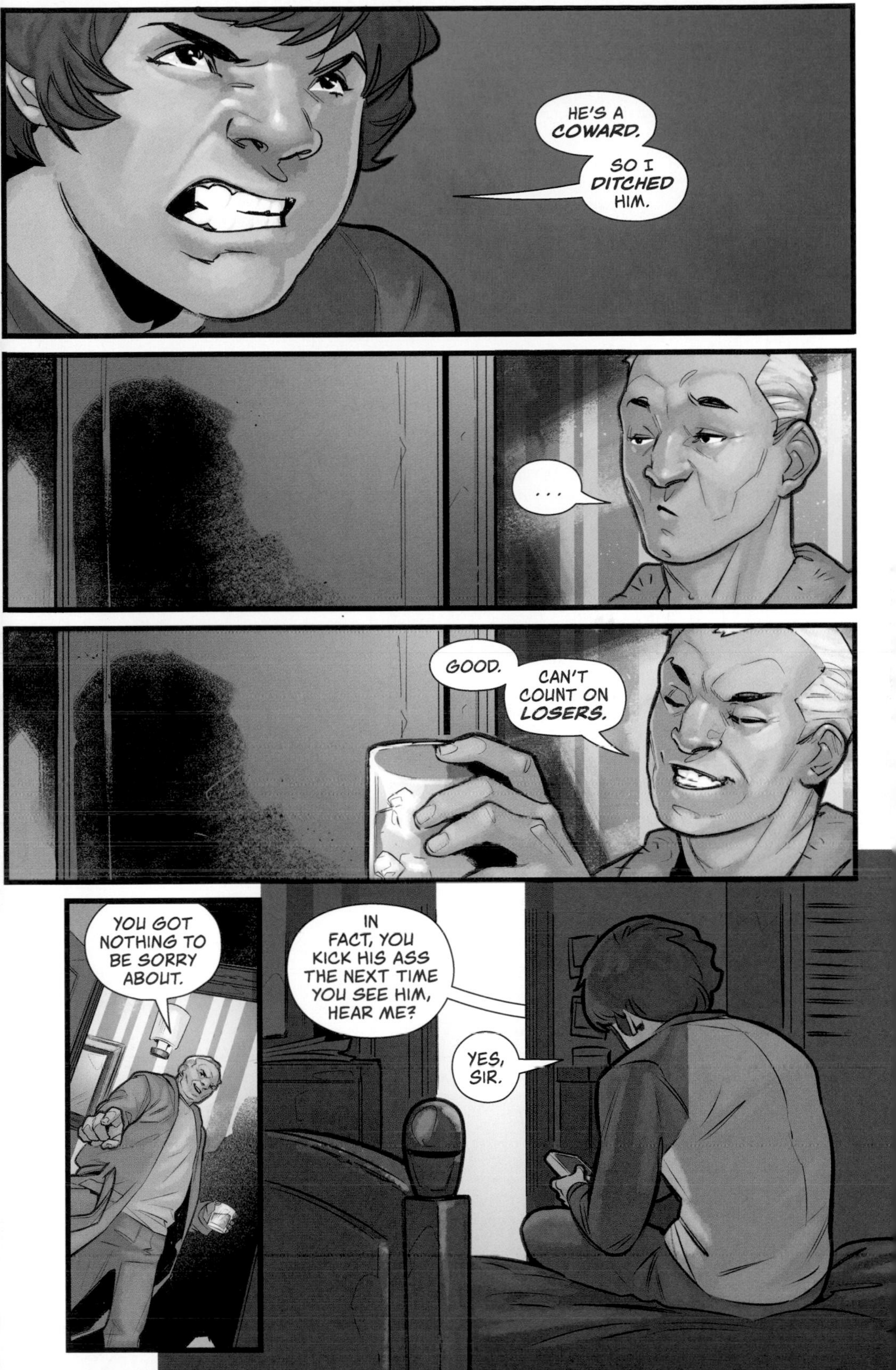
HE'S A COWARD.
SO I DITCHED HIM.
. . .
GOOD.
CAN'T COUNT ON LOSERS.
YOU GOT NOTHING TO BE SORRY ABOUT.
IN FACT, YOU KICK HIS ASS THE NEXT TIME YOU SEE HIM, HEAR ME?
YES, SIR.

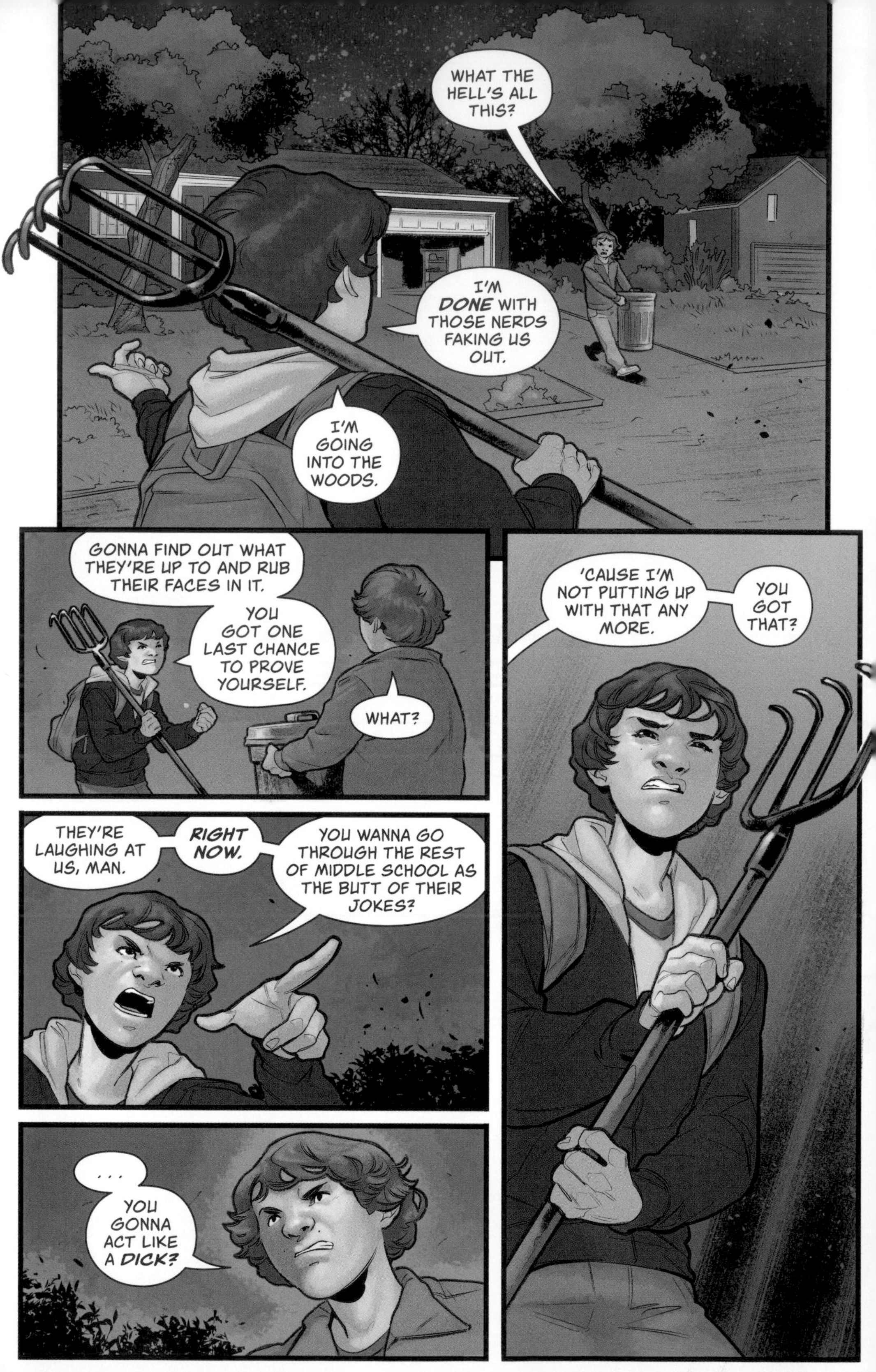
WHAT THE HELL'S ALL THIS?
I'M DONE WITH THOSE NERDS FAKING US OUT.
I'M GOING INTO THE WOODS.
GONNA FIND OUT WHAT THEY'RE UP TO AND RUB THEIR FACES IN IT.
YOU GOT ONE LAST CHANCE TO PROVE YOURSELF.
WHAT?
THEY'RE LAUGHING AT US, MAN.
RIGHT NOW.
YOU WANNA GO THROUGH THE REST OF MIDDLE SCHOOL AS THE BUTT OF THEIR JOKES?
...
YOU GONNA ACT LIKE A DICK?
'CAUSE I'M NOT PUTTING UP WITH THAT ANY MORE.
YOU GOT THAT?

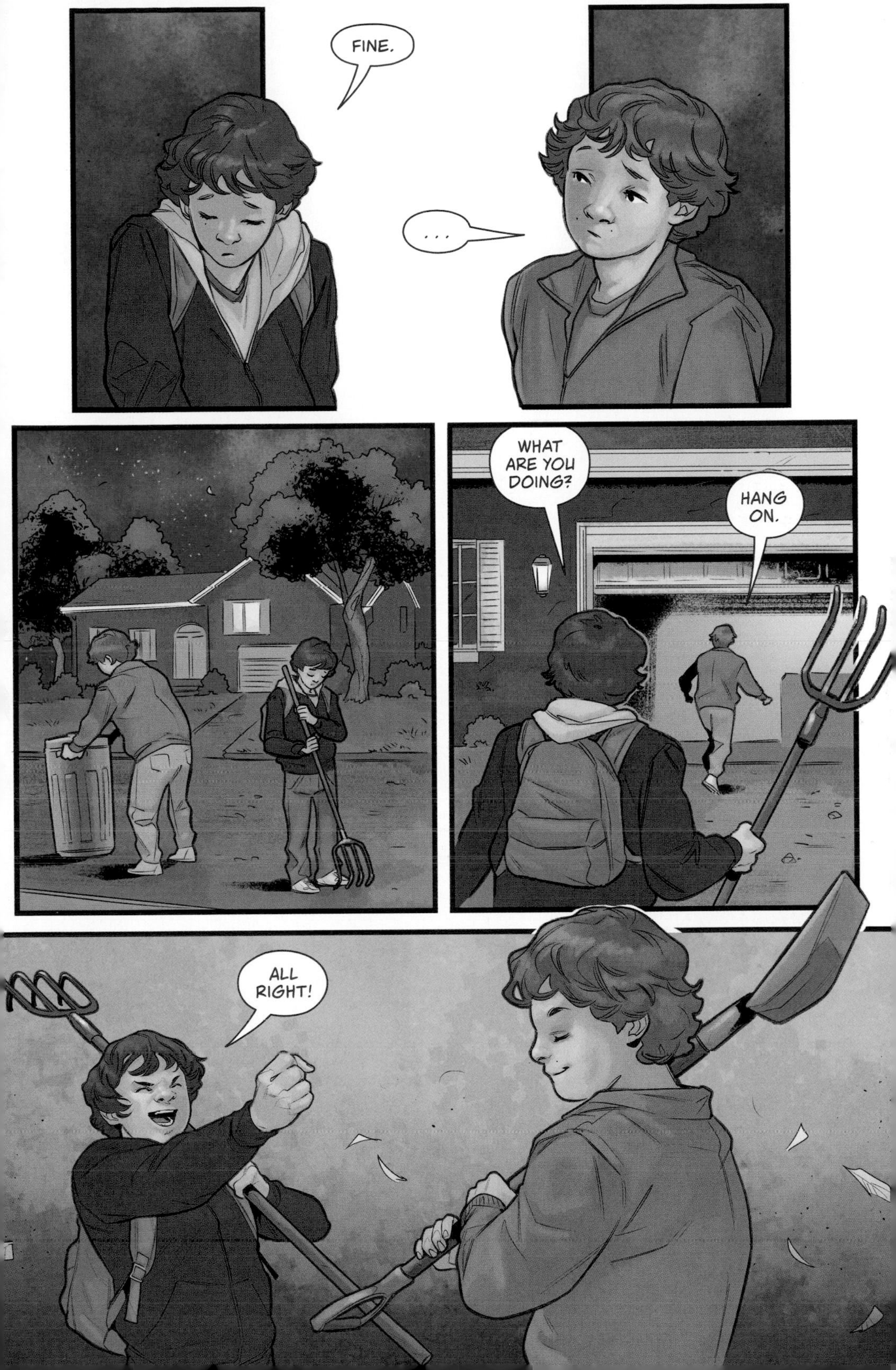
FINE.
...
WHAT ARE YOU DOING?
HANG ON.
ALL RIGHT!

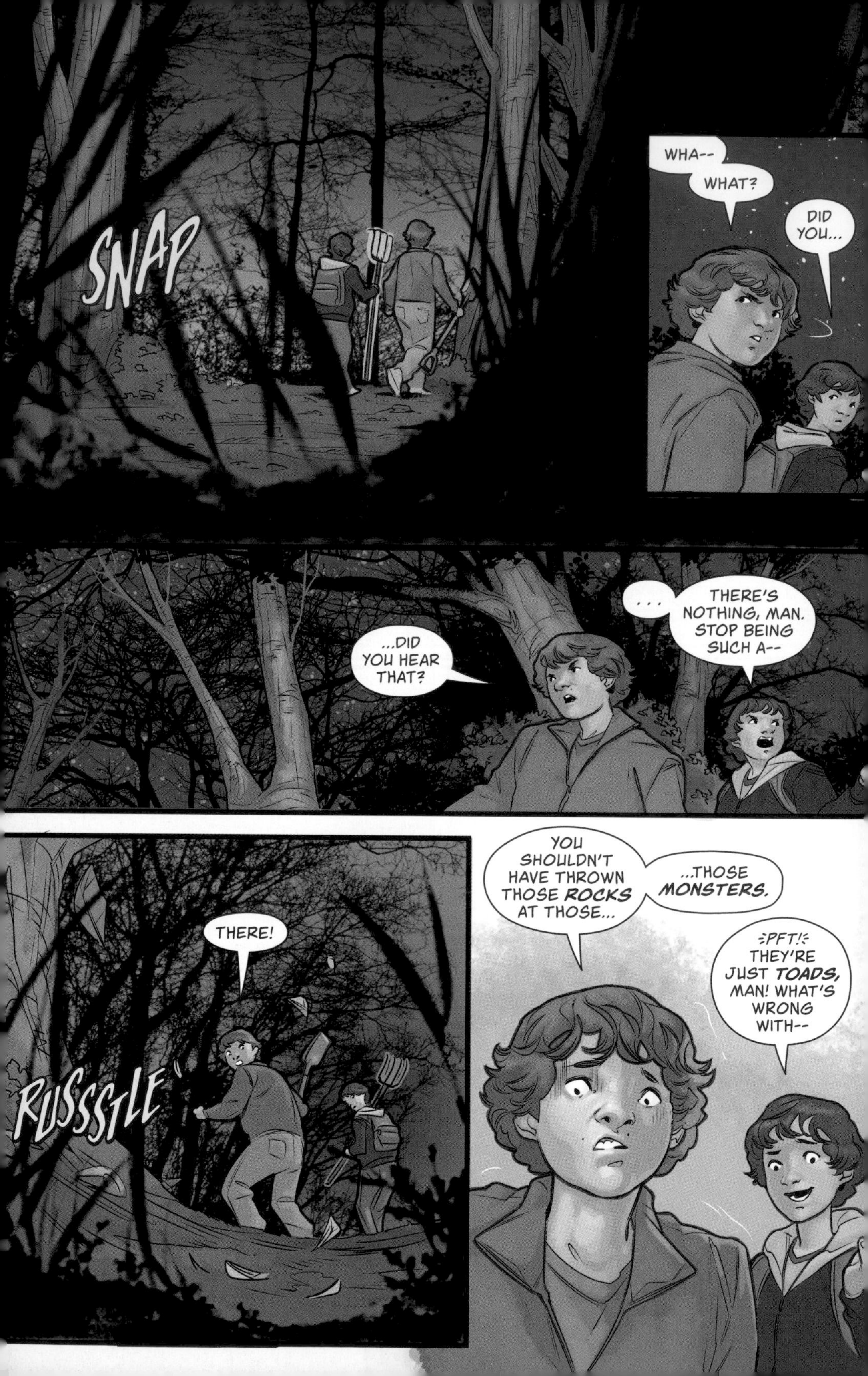
SNAP
WHA--
WHAT?
DID YOU...
...DID YOU HEAR THAT?
...
THERE'S NOTHING, MAN. STOP BEING SUCH A--
THERE!
RUSSSTLE
YOU SHOULDN'T HAVE THROWN THOSE ROCKS AT THOSE...
...THOSE MONSTERS.
PFT! THEY'RE JUST TOADS, MAN! WHAT'S WRONG WITH--

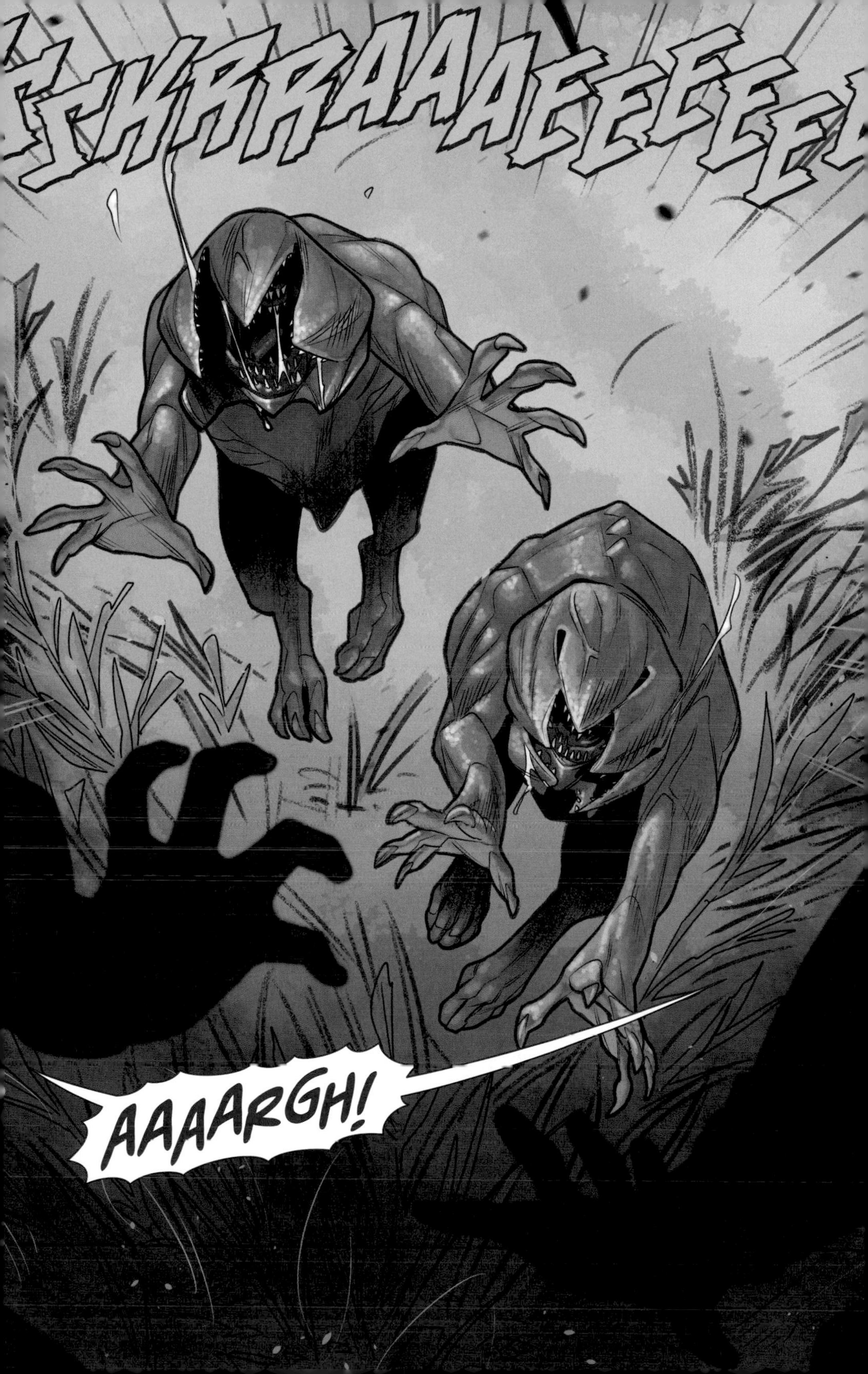
KRRAAAEEE
AAAARGH!

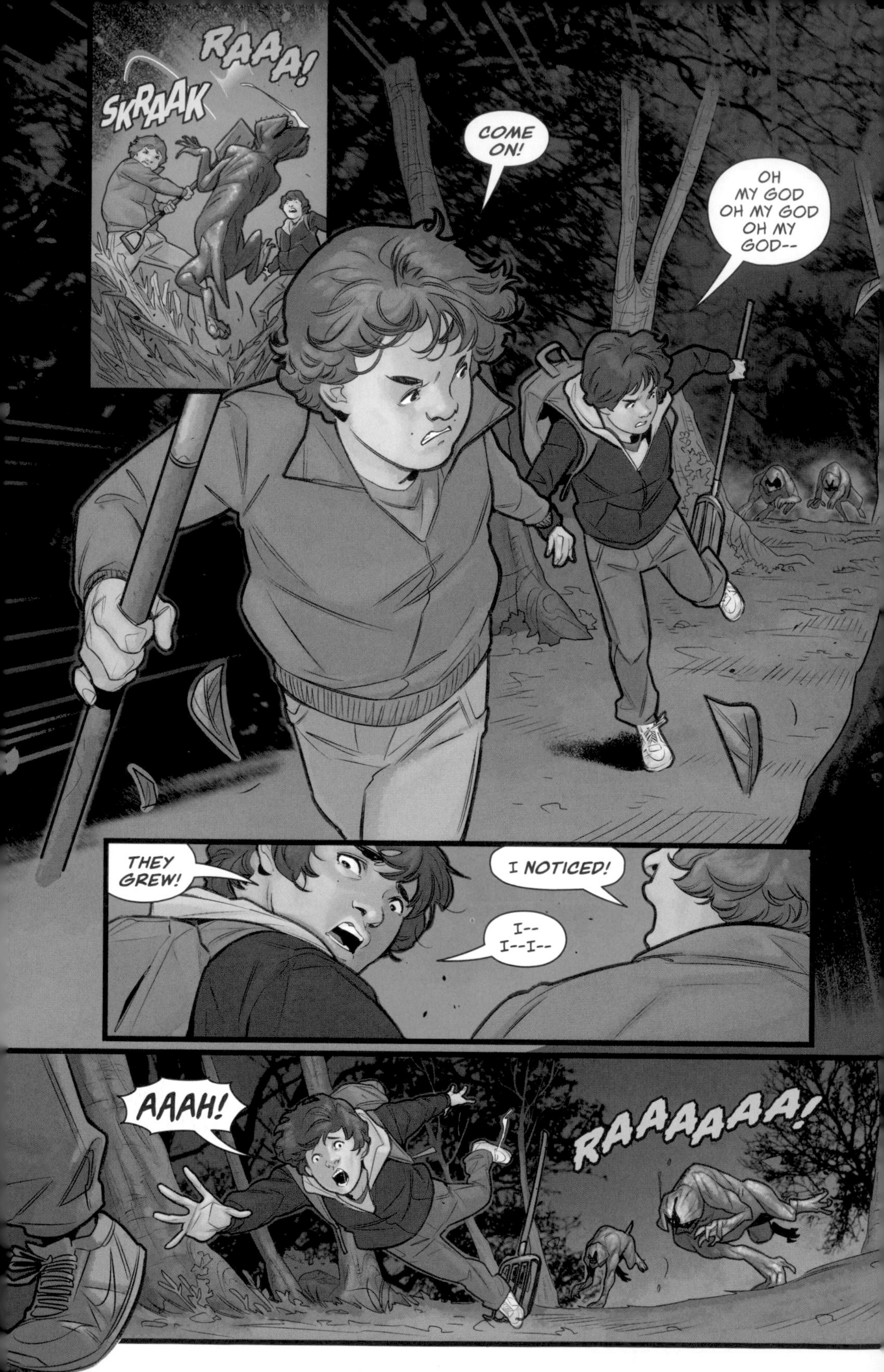
RAAA!
SKRAAK
COME ON!
OH MY GOD OH MY GOD OH MY GOD--
THEY GREW!
I NOTICED!
I-- I--I--
AAAH!
RAAAAAA!

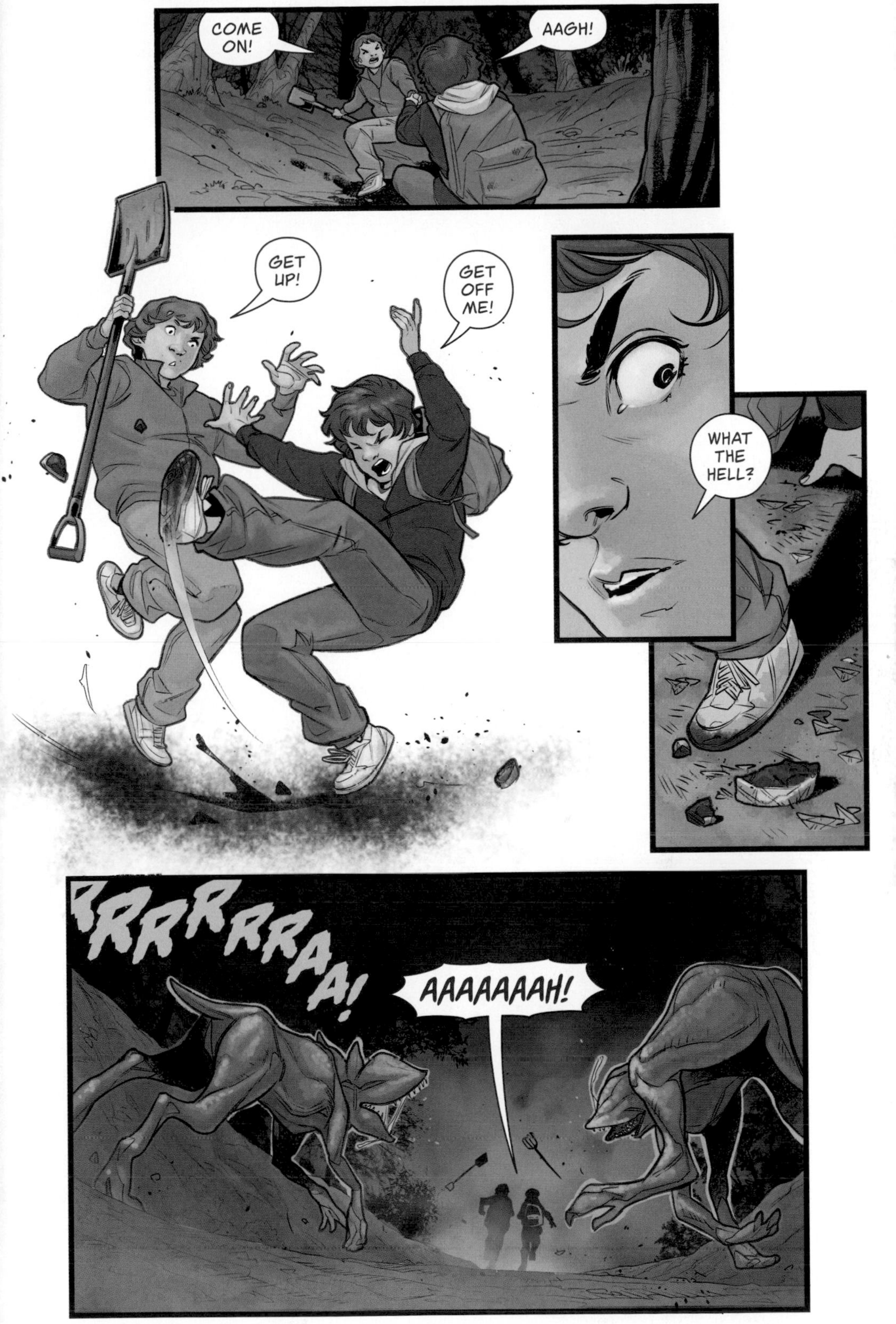
COME ON!
AAGH!
GET UP!
GET OFF ME!
WHAT THE HELL?
RRRRRRAA!
AAAAAAAH!

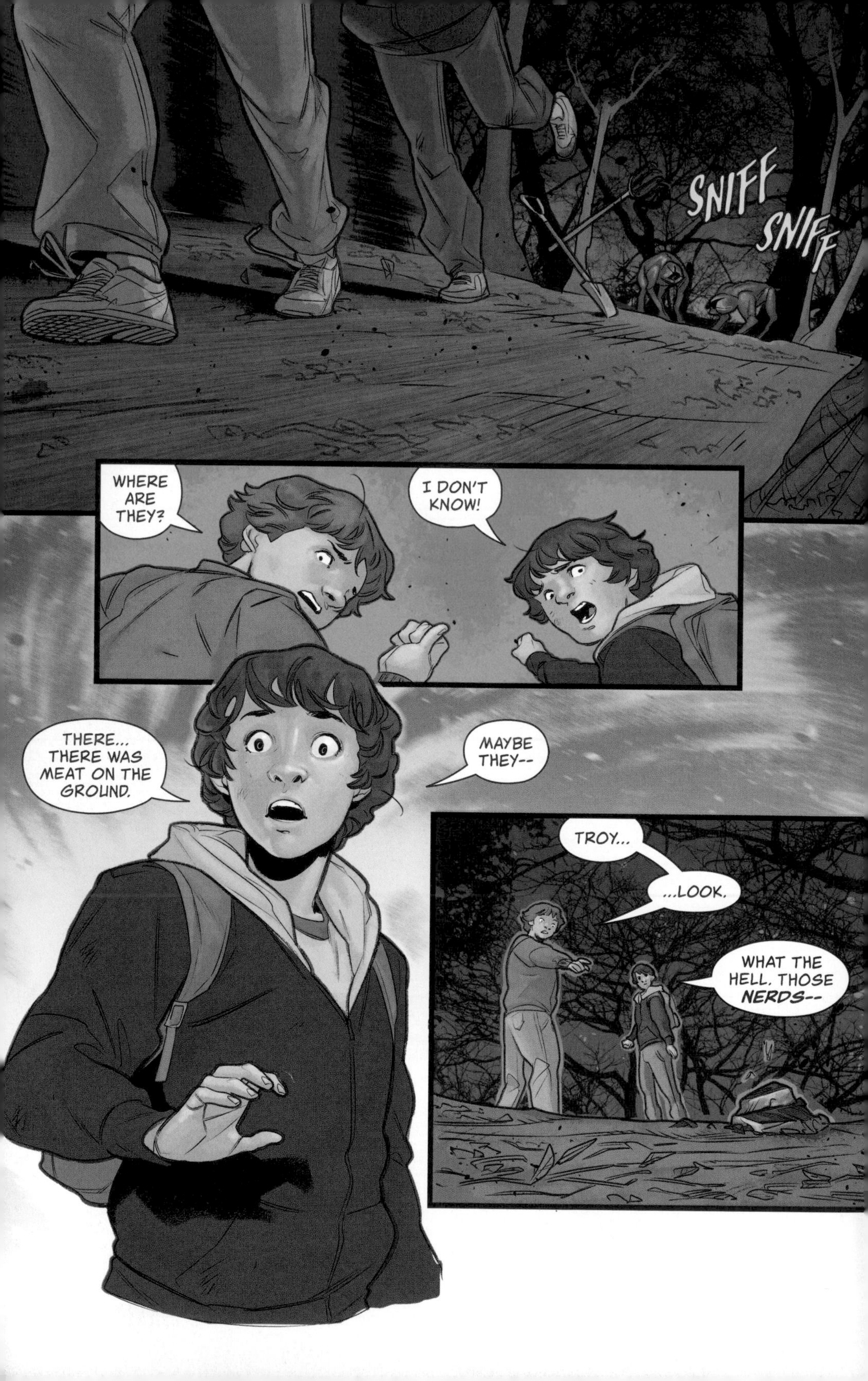

SNIFF
SNIFF
WHERE ARE THEY?
I DON'T KNOW!
THERE... THERE WAS MEAT ON THE GROUND.
MAYBE THEY--
TROY...
...LOOK.
WHAT THE HELL. THOSE *NERDS--*

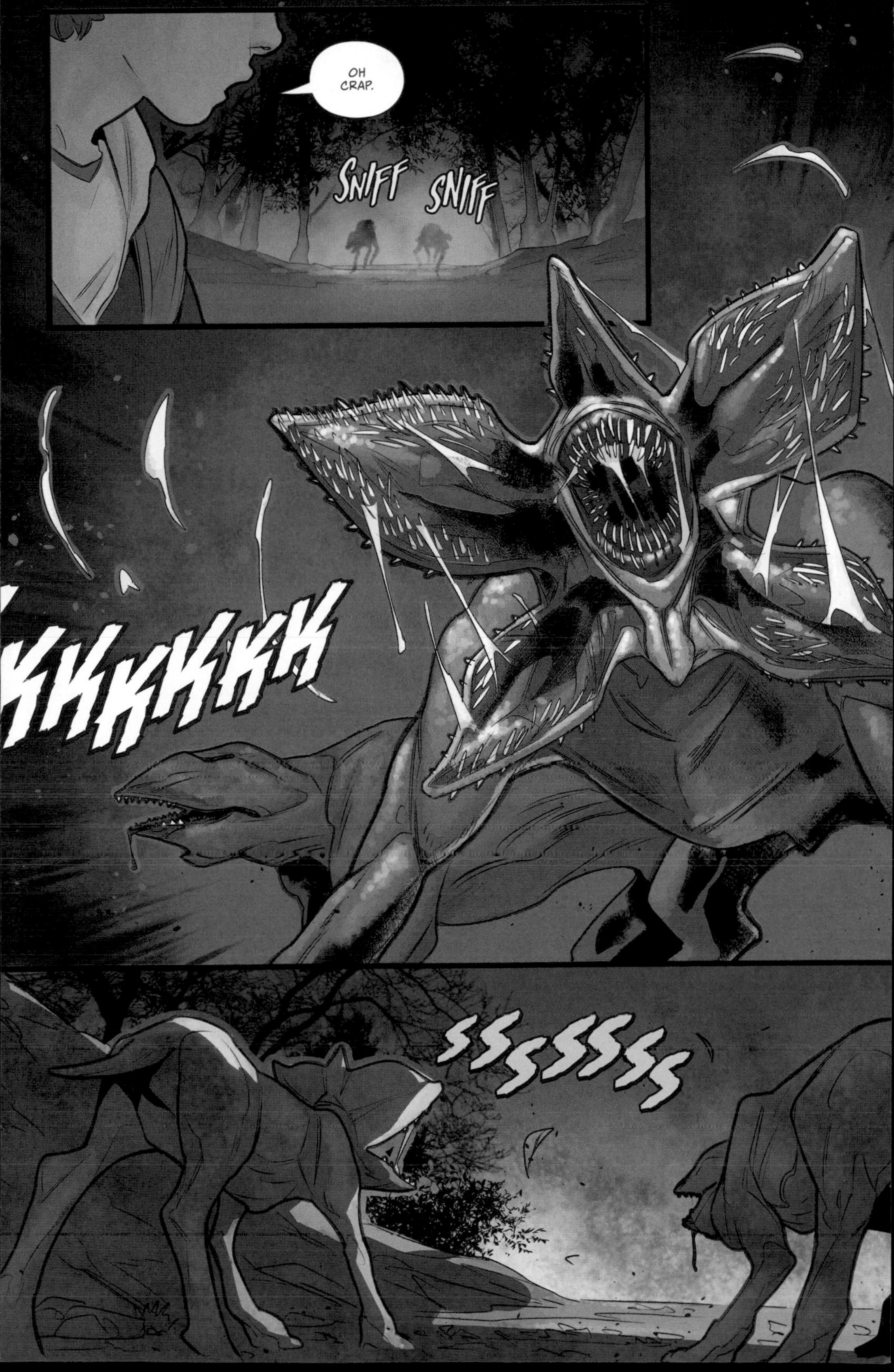
OH CRAP.
SNIFF SNIFF
KKKKKKK
SSSSSSS

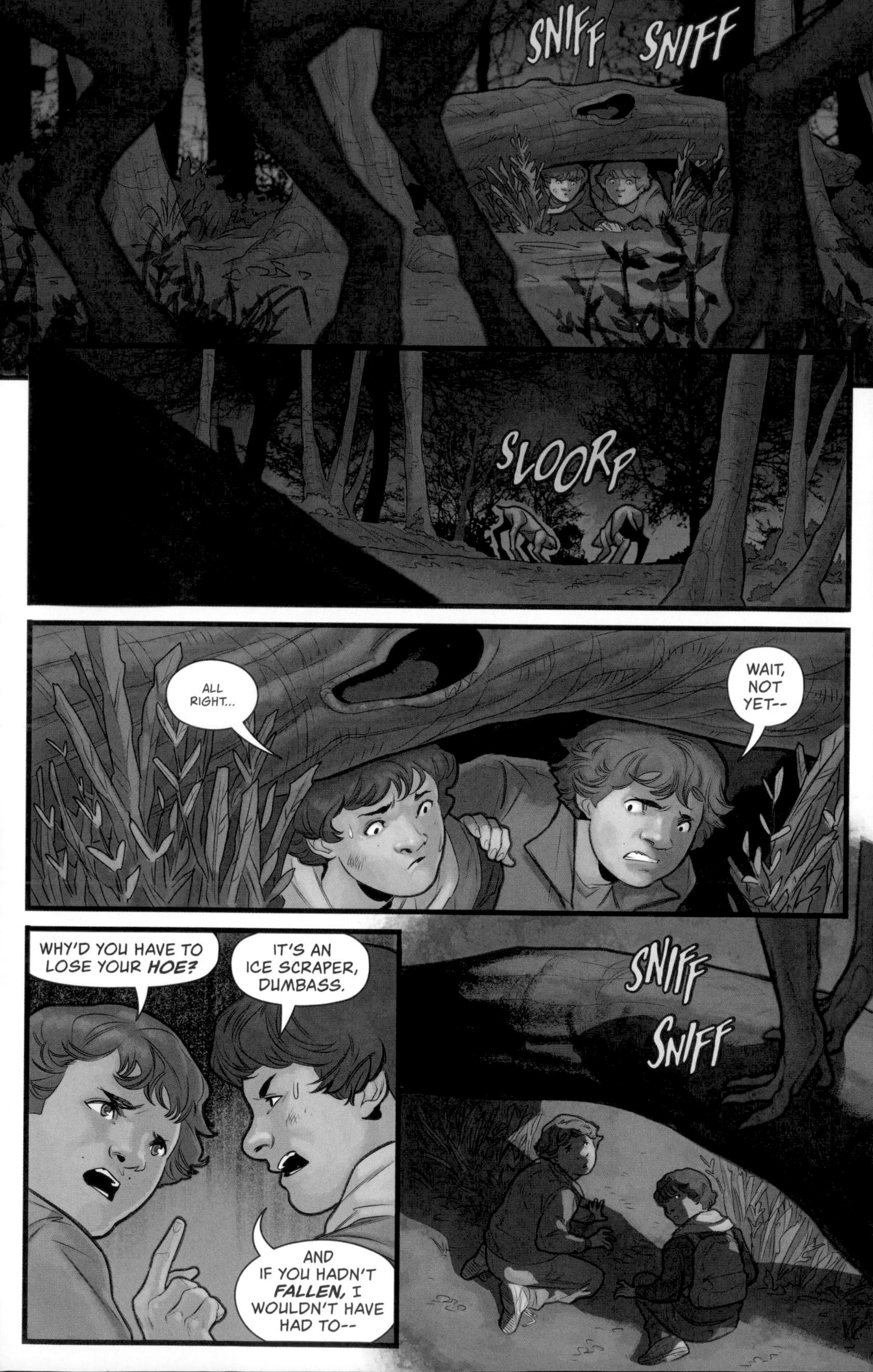
SNIFF SNIFF
SLOORP
ALL RIGHT...
WAIT, NOT YET--
SNIFF
SNIFF
WHY'D YOU HAVE TO LOSE YOUR HOE?
IT'S AN ICE SCRAPER, DUMBASS.
AND IF YOU HADN'T FALLEN, I WOULDN'T HAVE HAD TO--

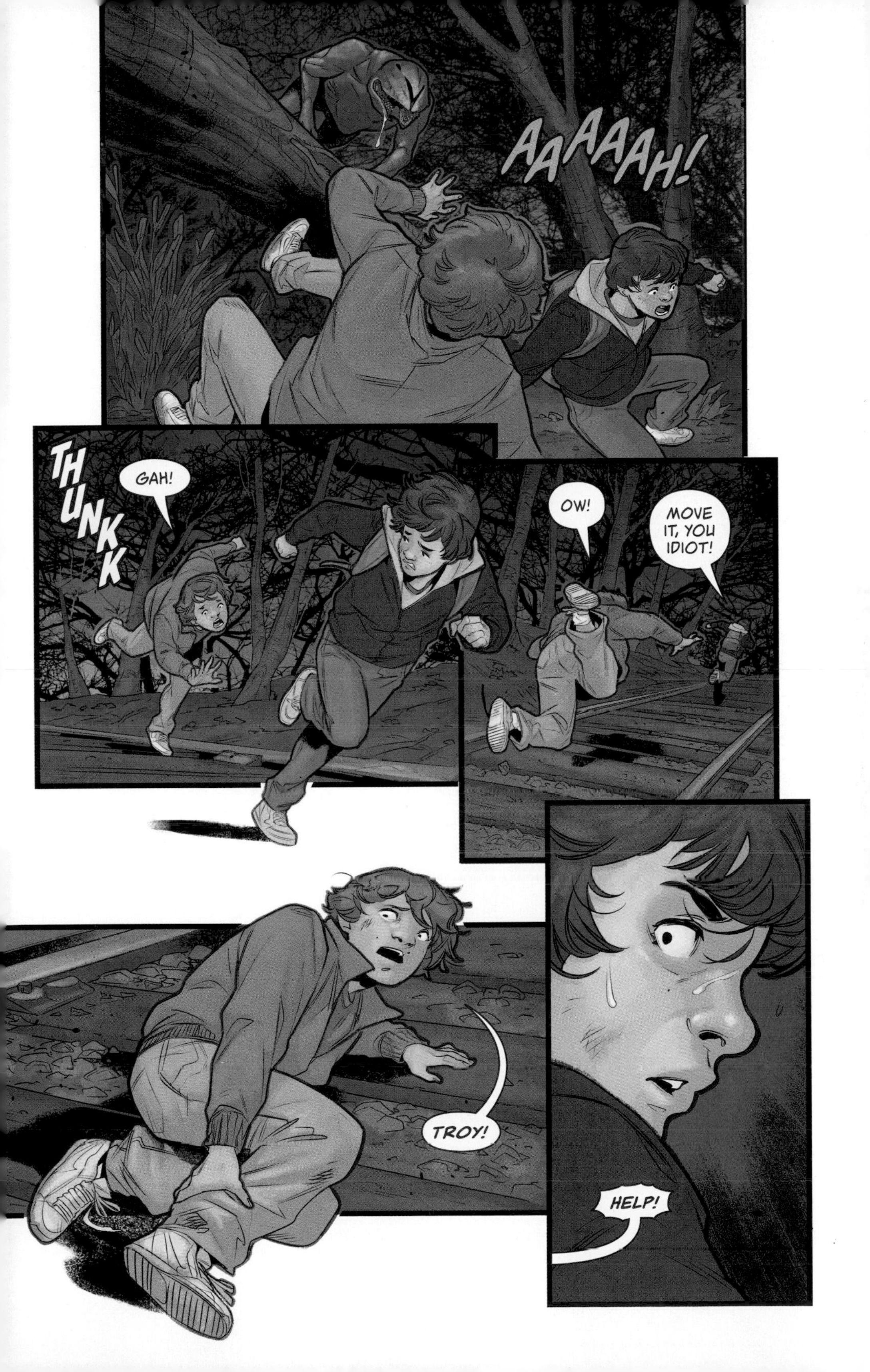
AAAAAH!
THUNKK
GAH!
OW!
MOVE IT, YOU IDIOT!
TROY!
HELP!

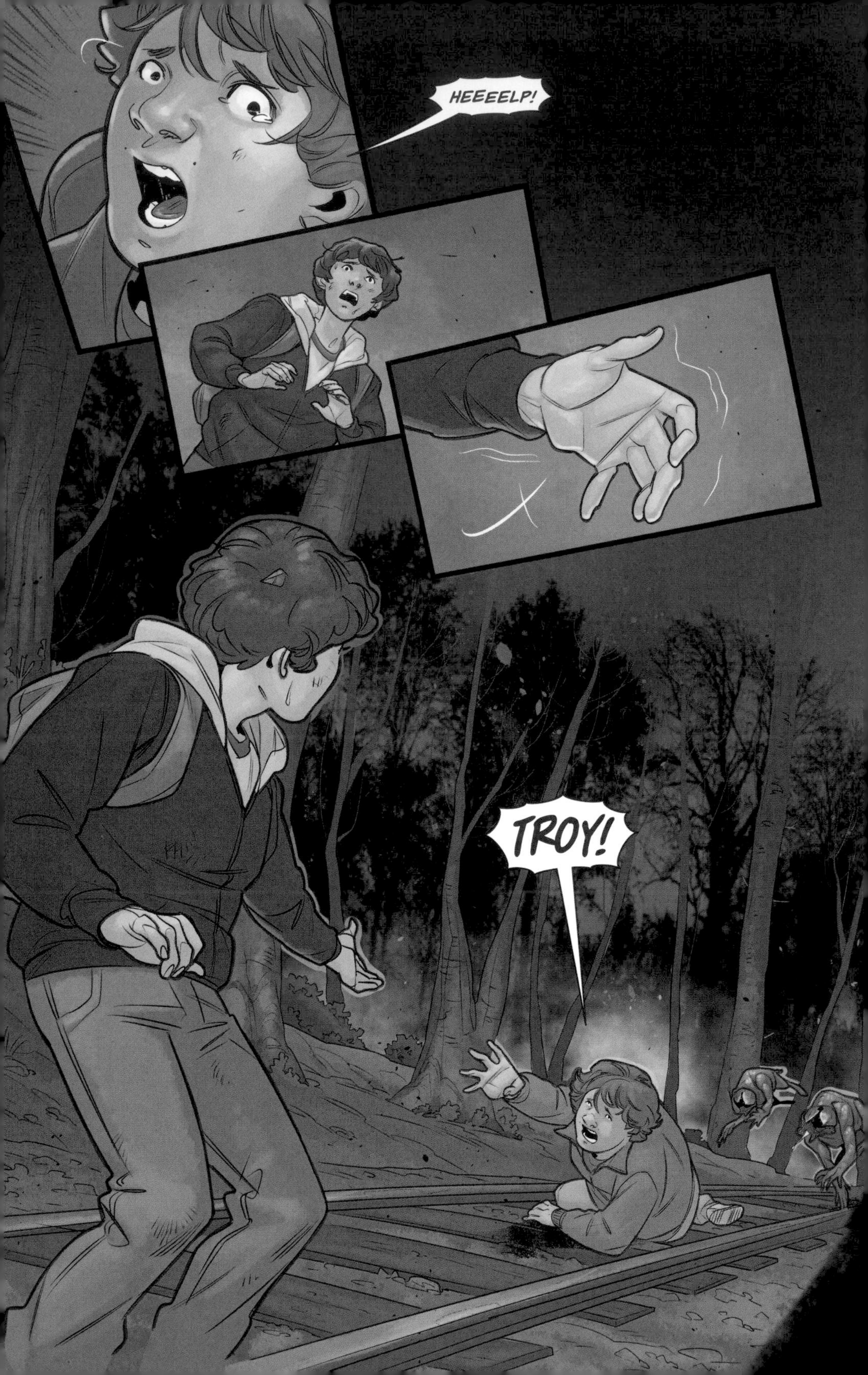
HEEEELP!
TROY!

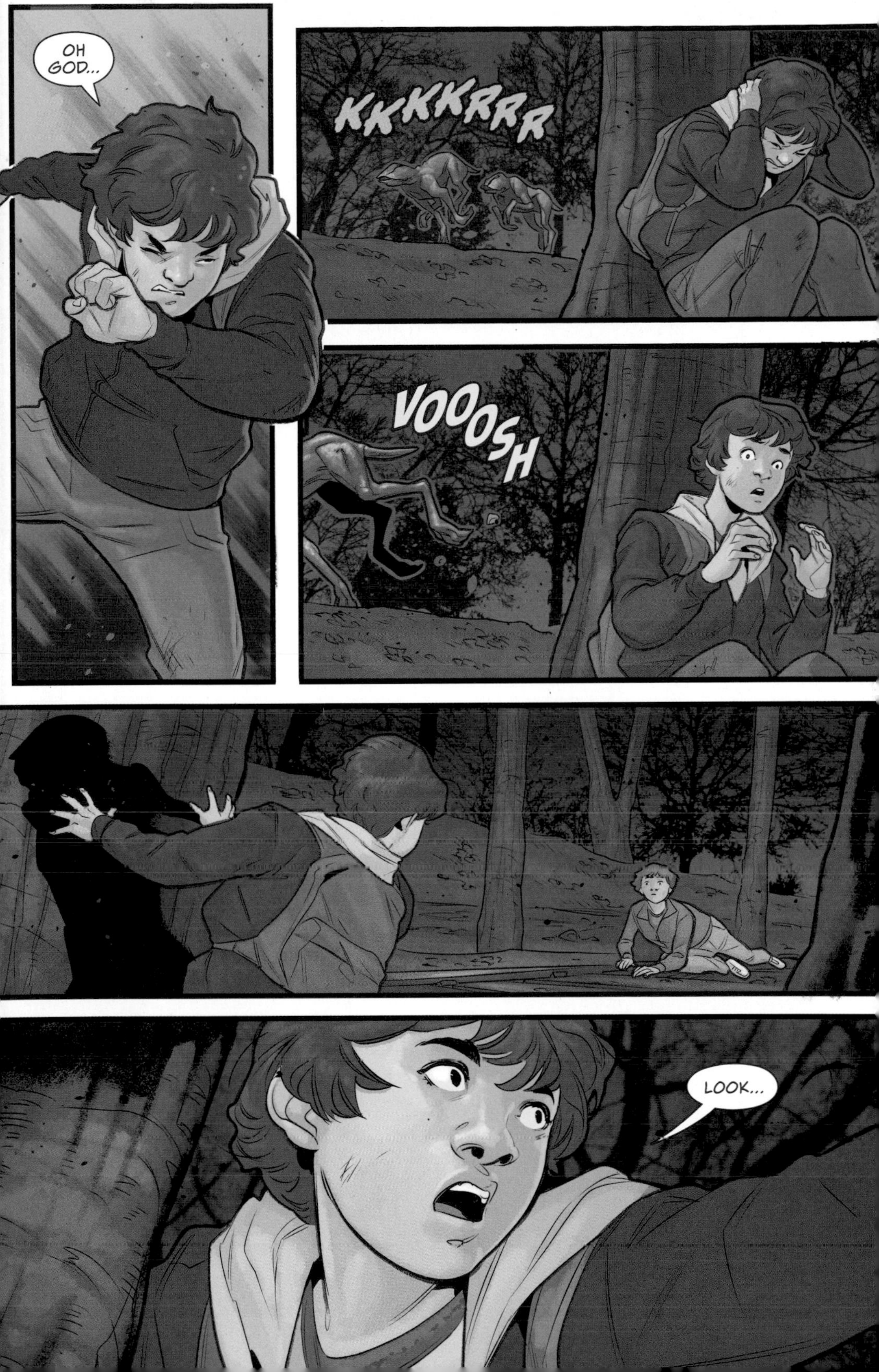
OH GOD...
KKKKRRRR
VOOOSH
LOOK...

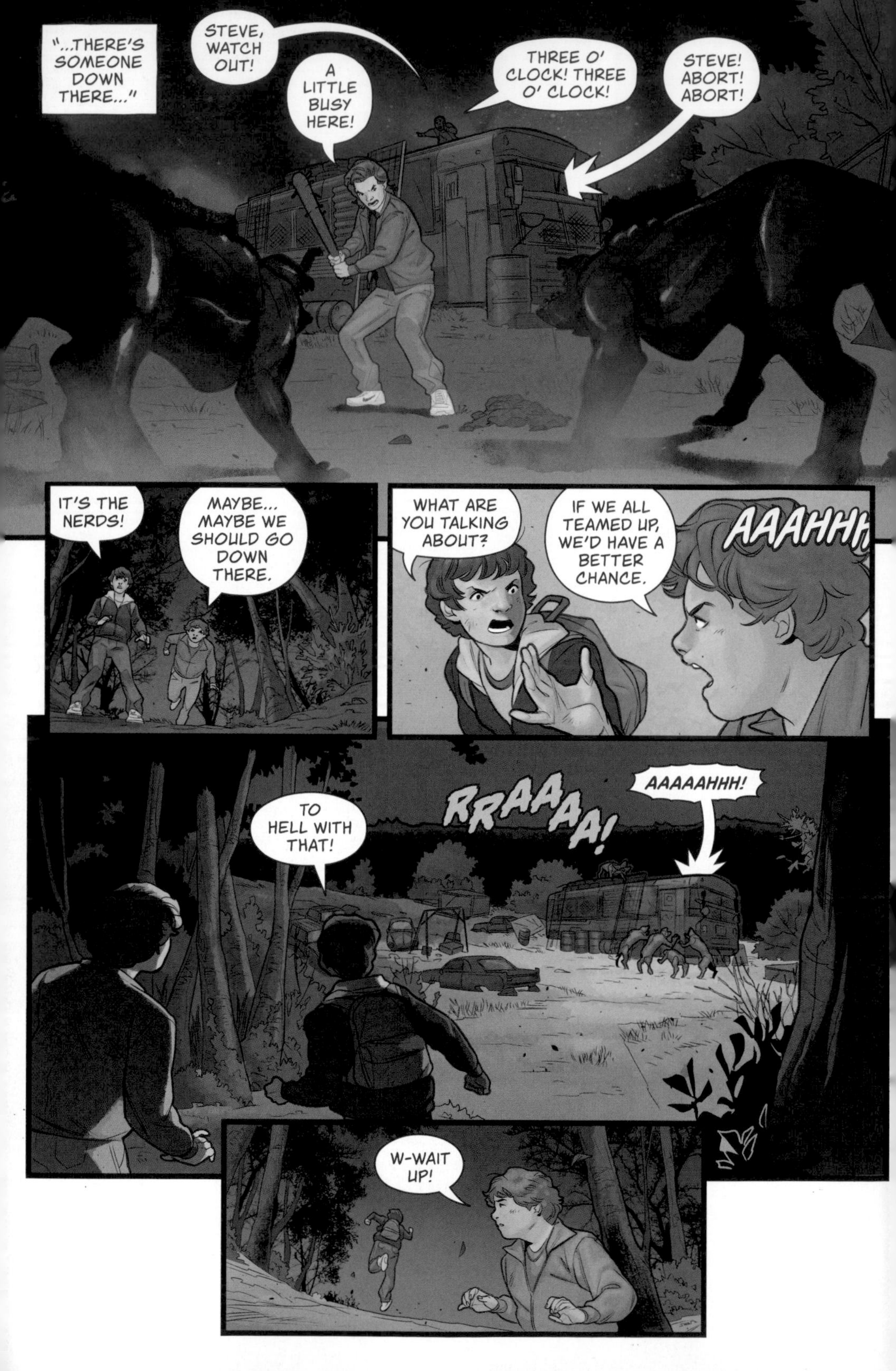
"...THERE'S SOMEONE DOWN THERE..."
STEVE, WATCH OUT!
A LITTLE BUSY HERE!
THREE O' CLOCK! THREE O' CLOCK!
STEVE! ABORT! ABORT!
IT'S THE NERDS!
MAYBE... MAYBE WE SHOULD GO DOWN THERE.
WHAT ARE YOU TALKING ABOUT?
IF WE ALL TEAMED UP, WE'D HAVE A BETTER CHANCE.
AAAHHH
TO HELL WITH THAT!
RRAAAAA!
AAAAAHHH!
W-WAIT UP!

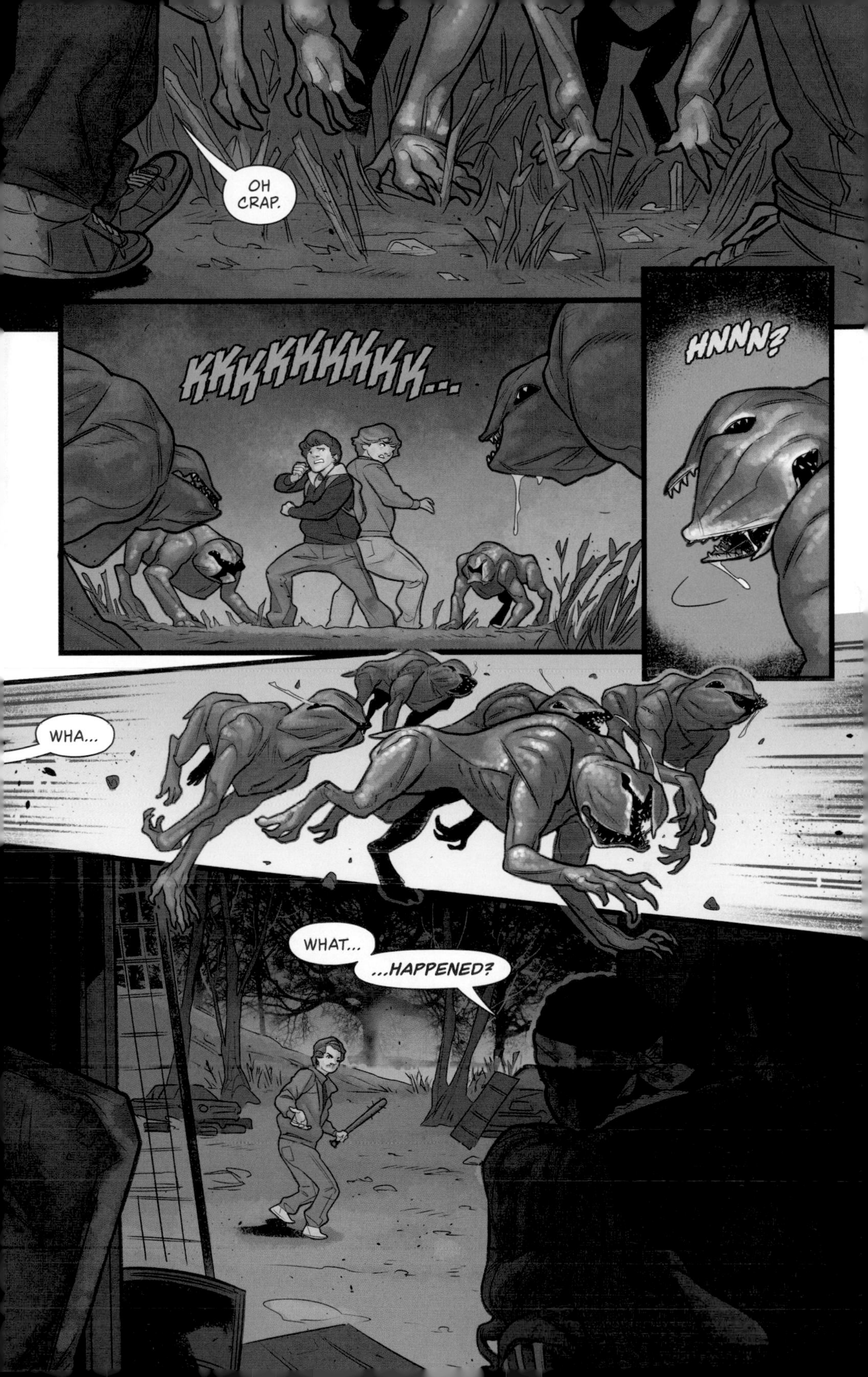

OH CRAP.
KKKKKKKKK...
HNNN?
WHA...
WHAT...
...HAPPENED?

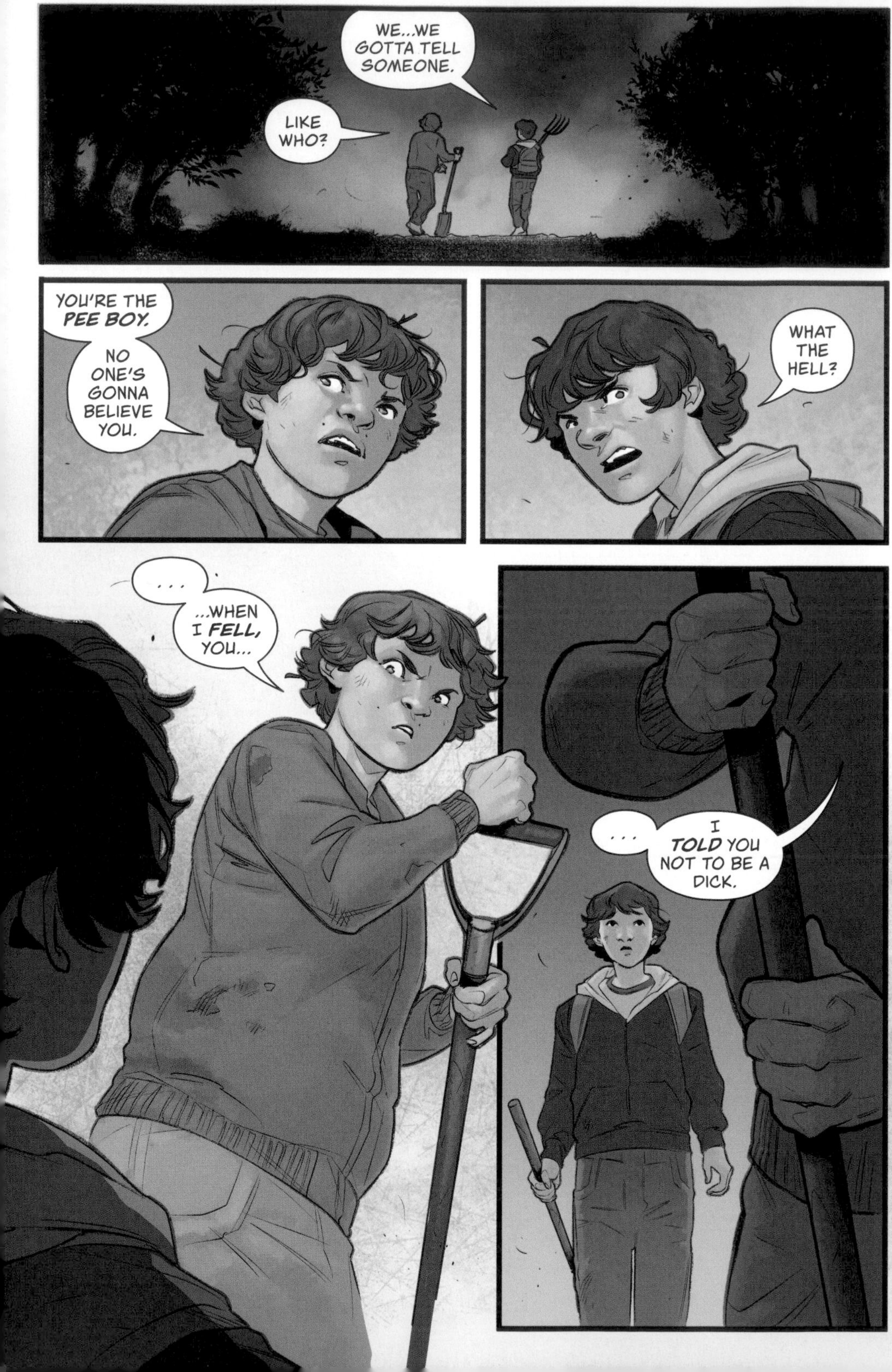
WE...WE GOTTA TELL SOMEONE.
LIKE WHO?
YOU'RE THE ***PEE BOY.***
NO ONE'S GONNA BELIEVE YOU.
WHAT THE HELL?
. . .
...WHEN I ***FELL,*** YOU...
. . .
I ***TOLD*** YOU NOT TO BE A DICK.

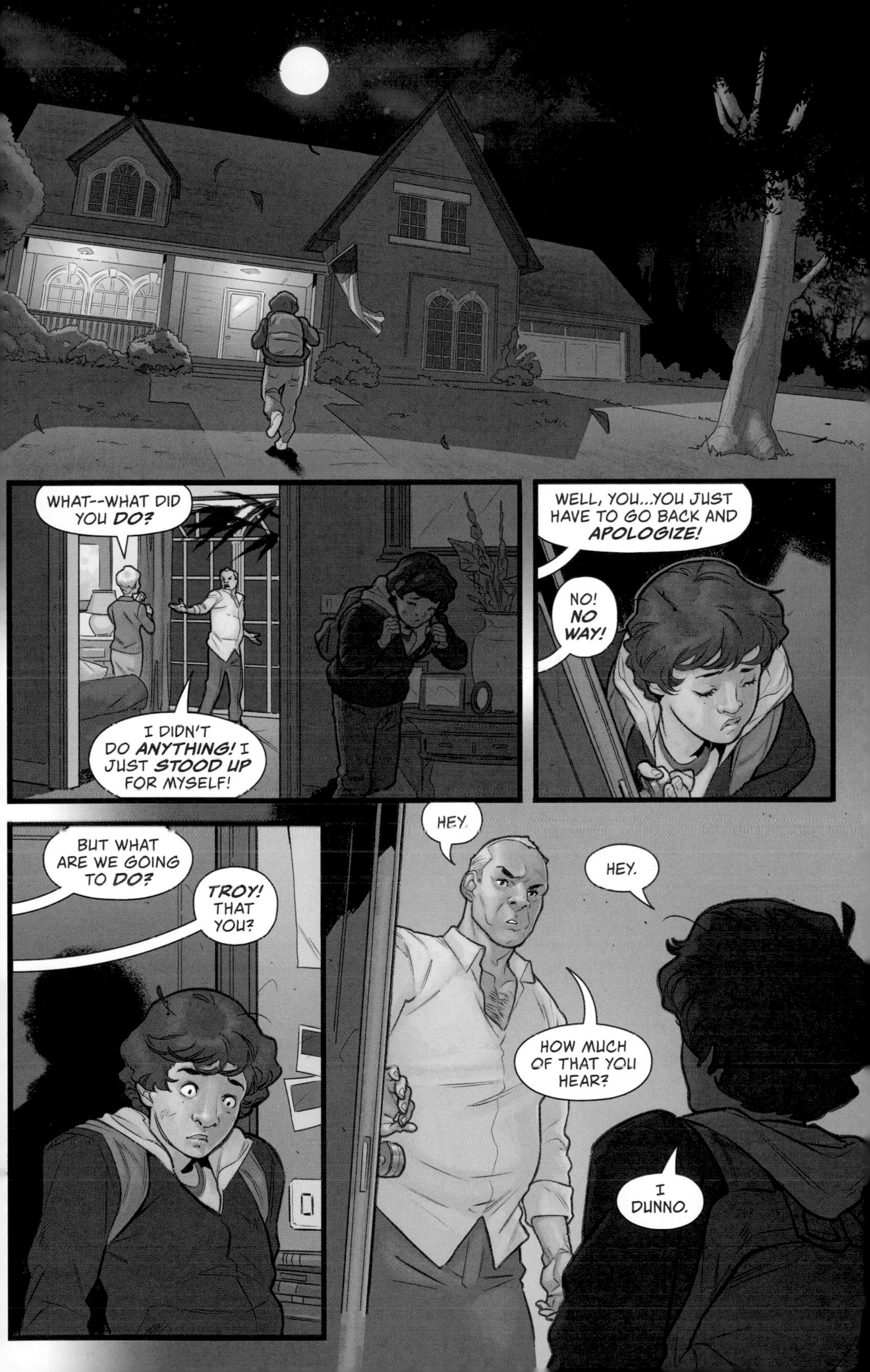
WHAT--WHAT DID YOU DO?
I DIDN'T DO ANYTHING! I JUST STOOD UP FOR MYSELF!
WELL, YOU...YOU JUST HAVE TO GO BACK AND APOLOGIZE!
NO! NO WAY!
BUT WHAT ARE WE GOING TO DO?
TROY! THAT YOU?
HEY.
HEY.
HOW MUCH OF THAT YOU HEAR?
I DUNNO.

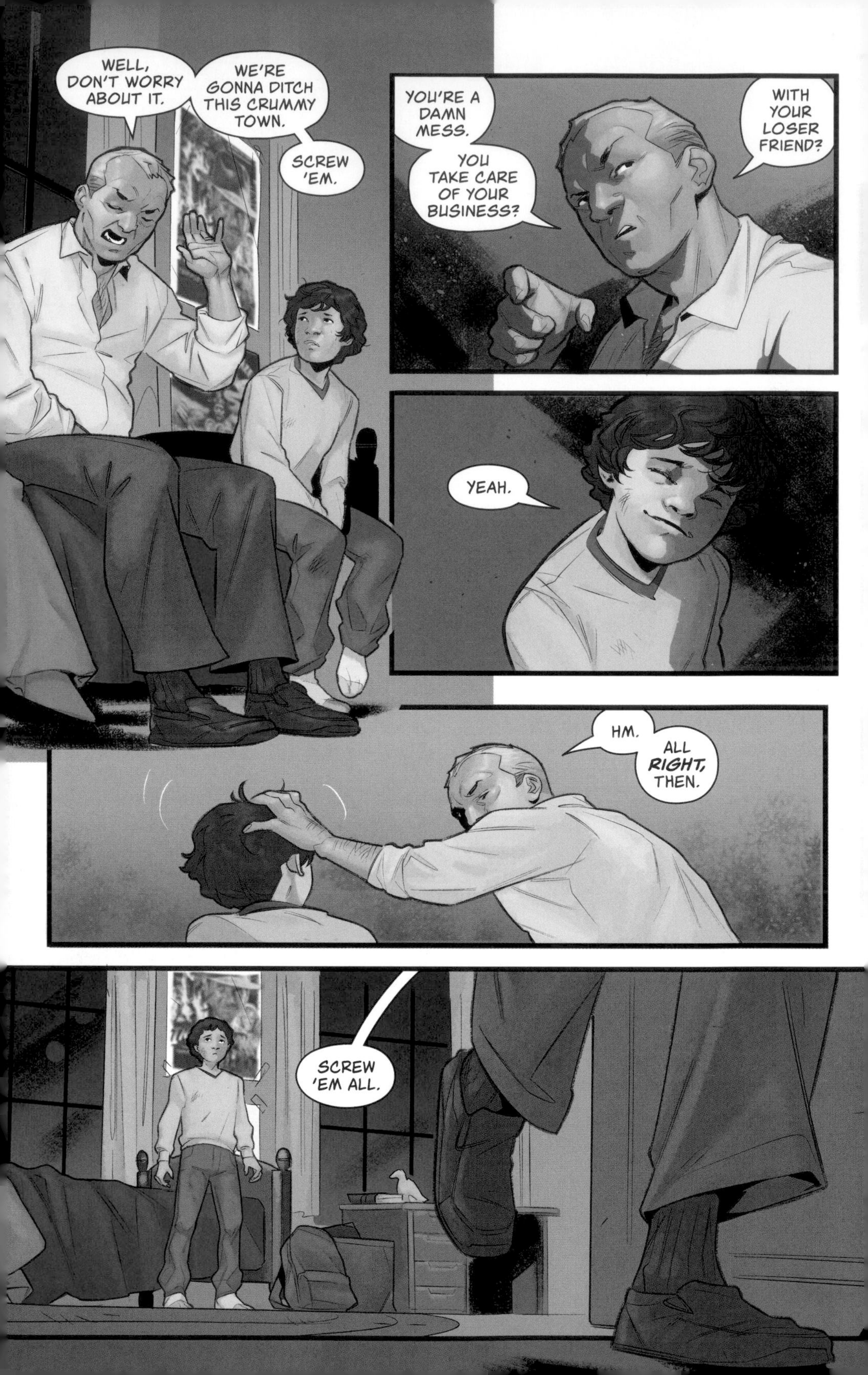
WELL, DON'T WORRY ABOUT IT.
WE'RE GONNA DITCH THIS CRUMMY TOWN.
SCREW 'EM.
YOU'RE A DAMN MESS.
YOU TAKE CARE OF YOUR BUSINESS?
WITH YOUR LOSER FRIEND?
YEAH.
HM.
ALL RIGHT, THEN.
SCREW 'EM ALL.

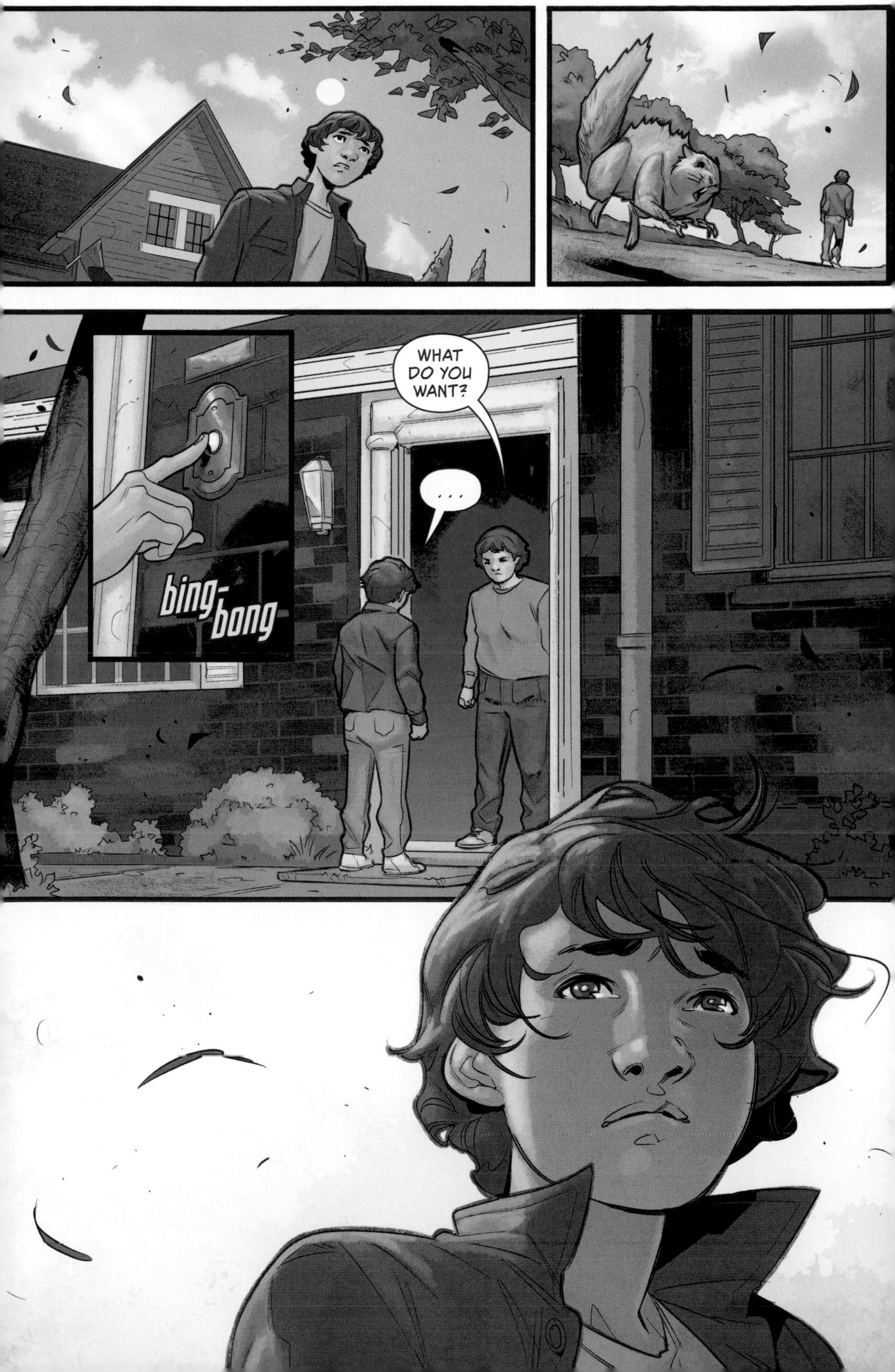
bing-bong
WHAT DO YOU WANT?
...

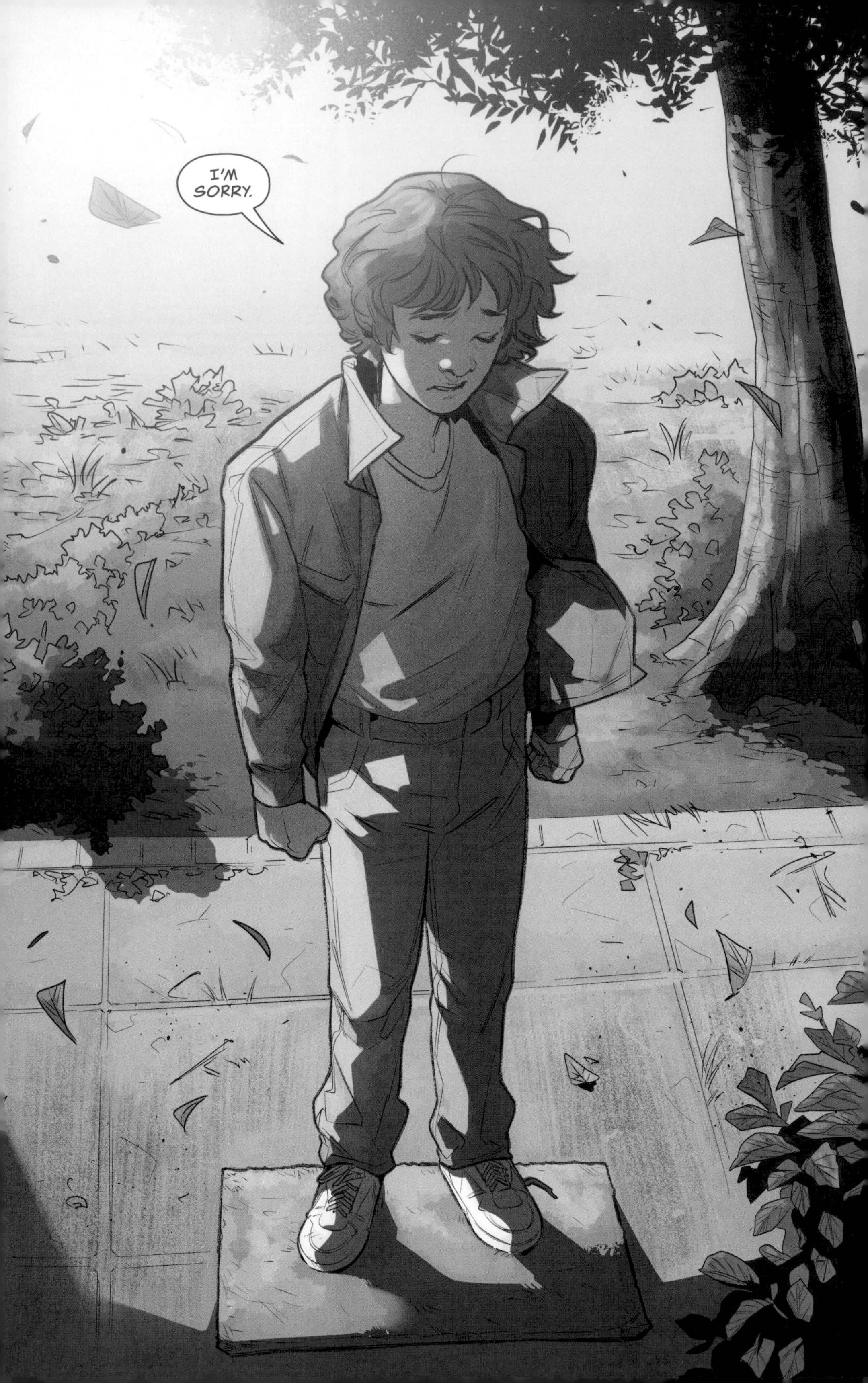
I'M SORRY.

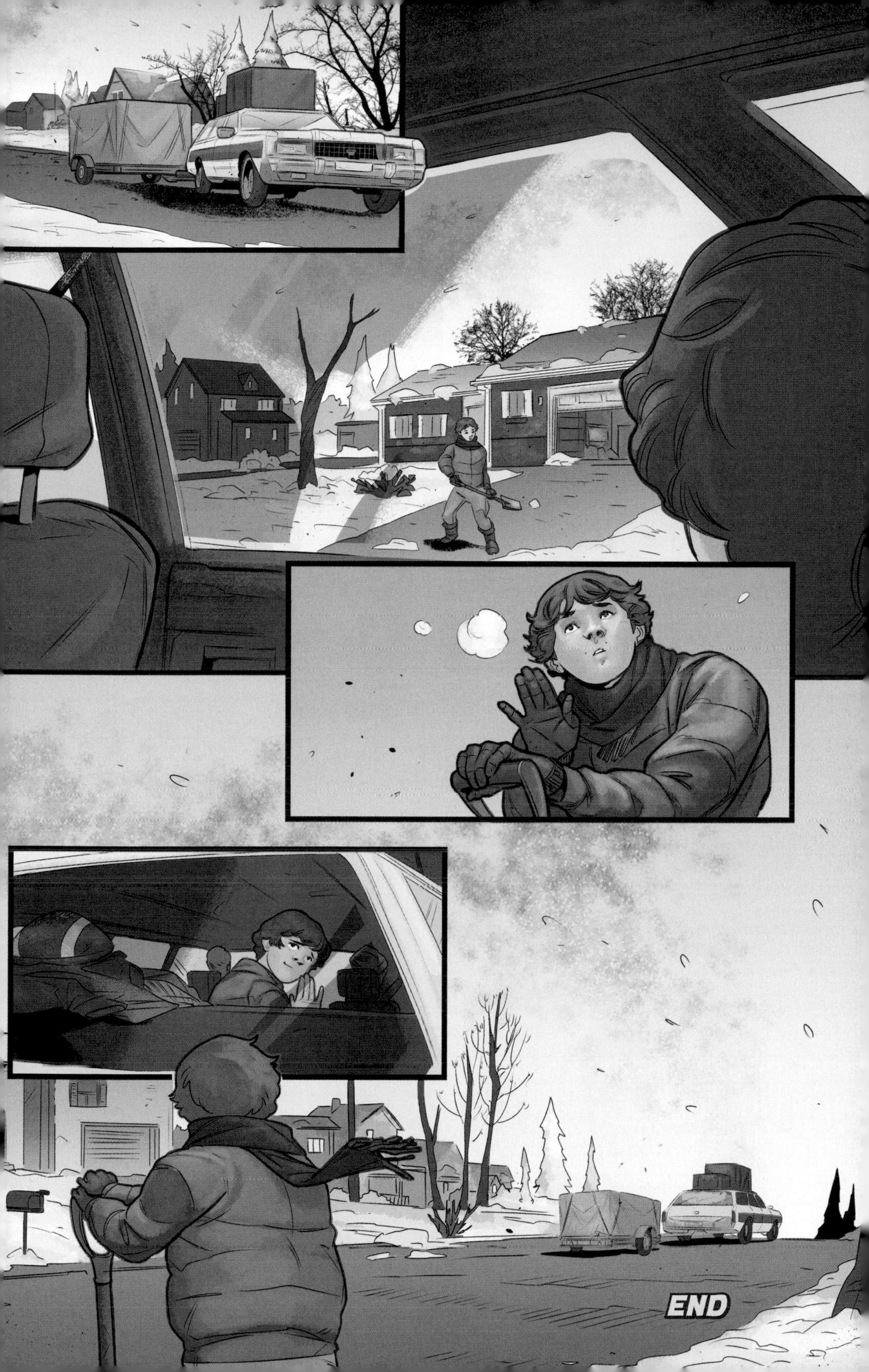
END

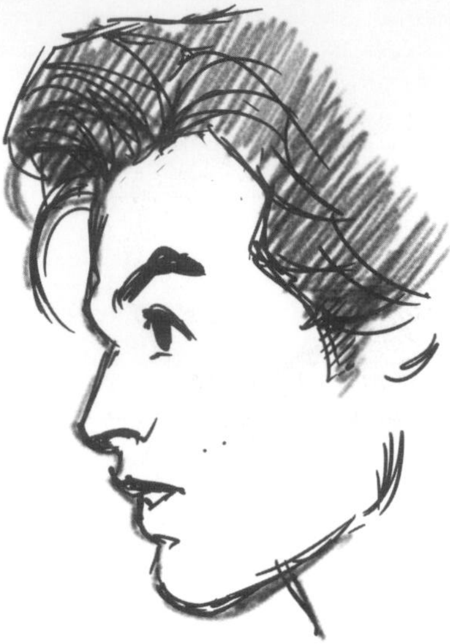

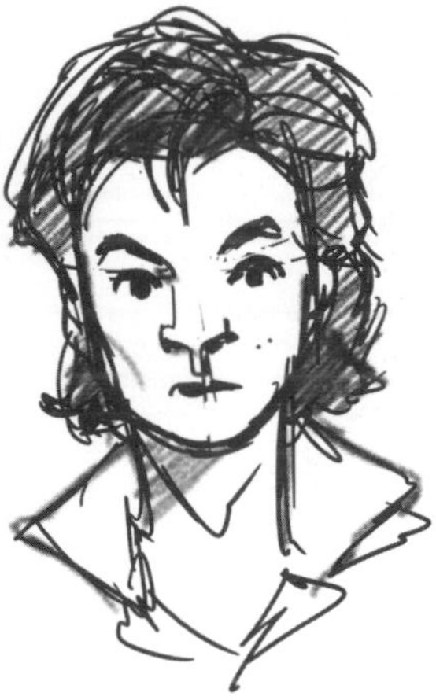

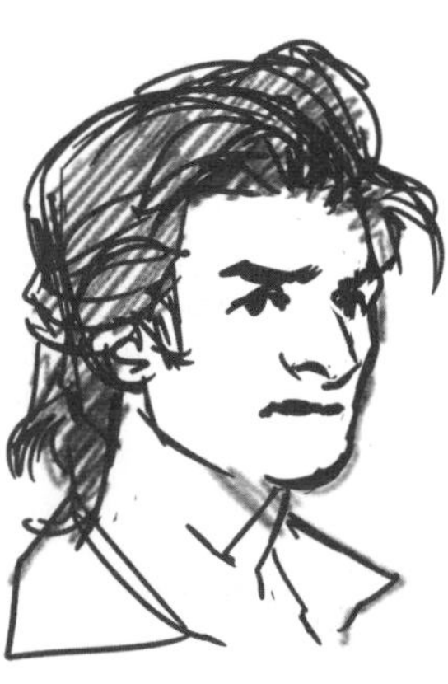

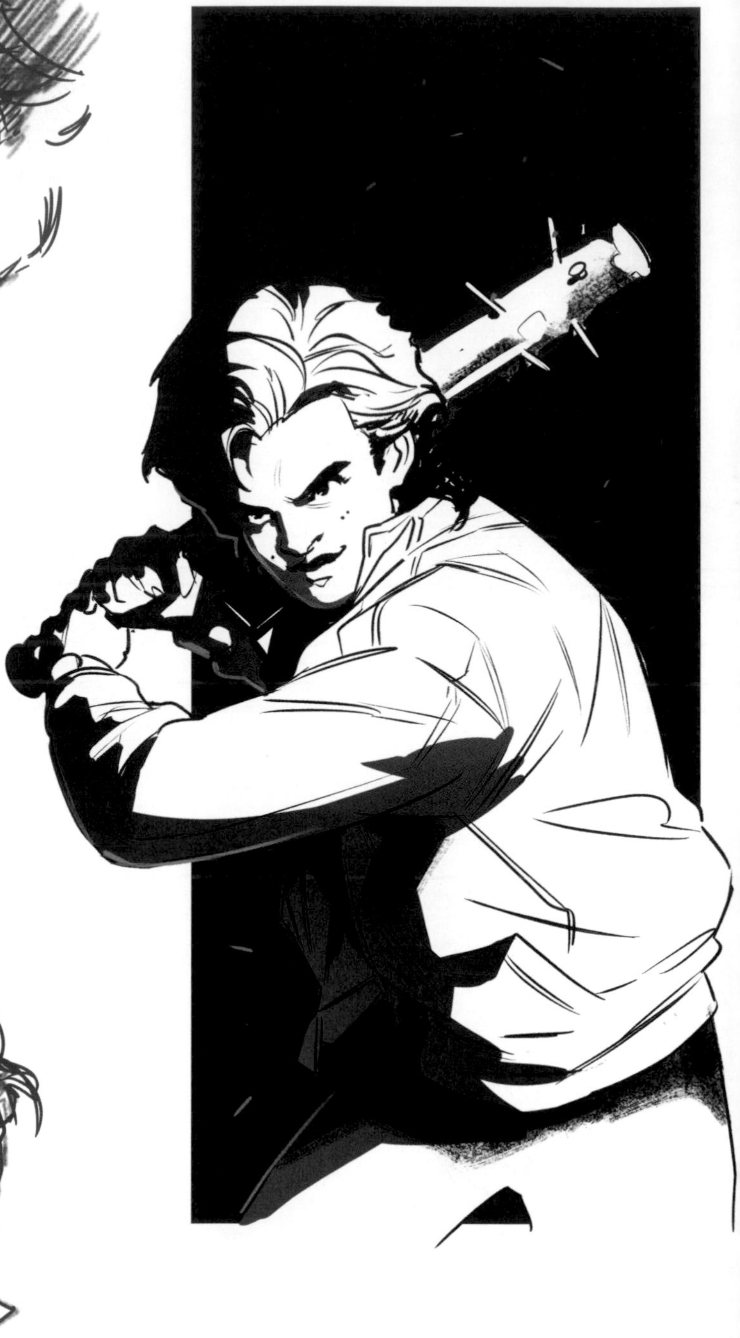

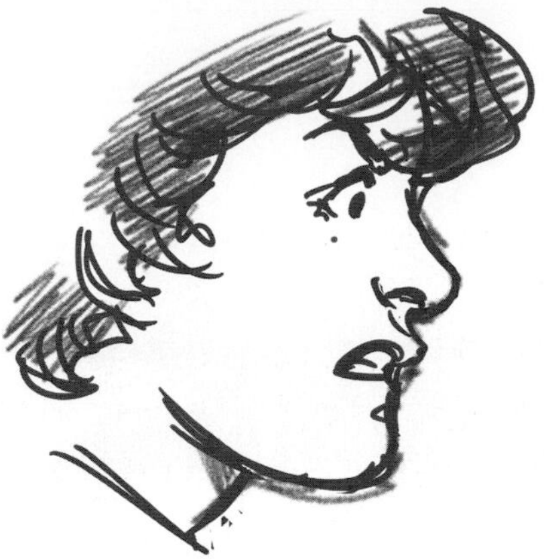
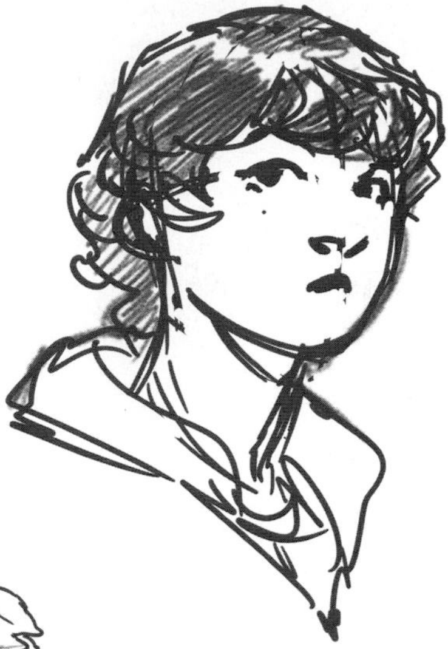
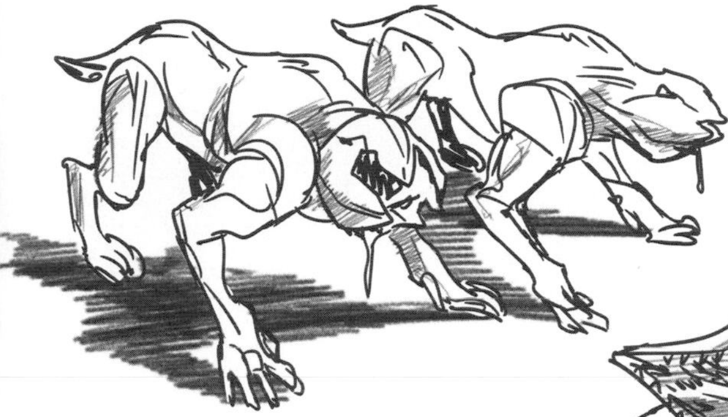
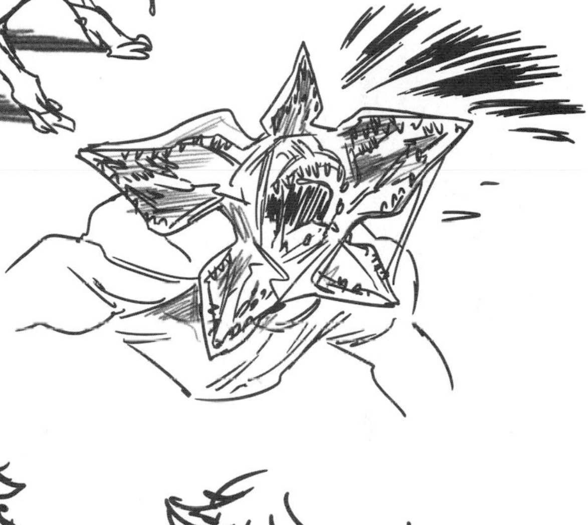
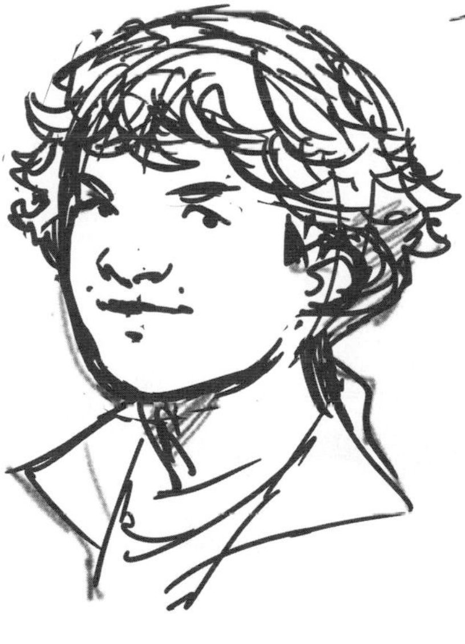
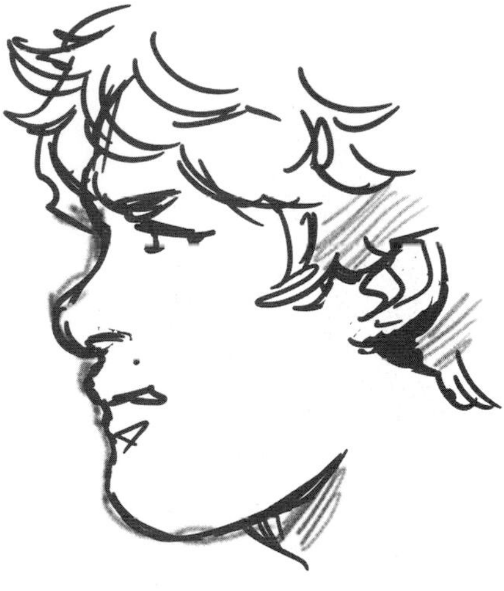

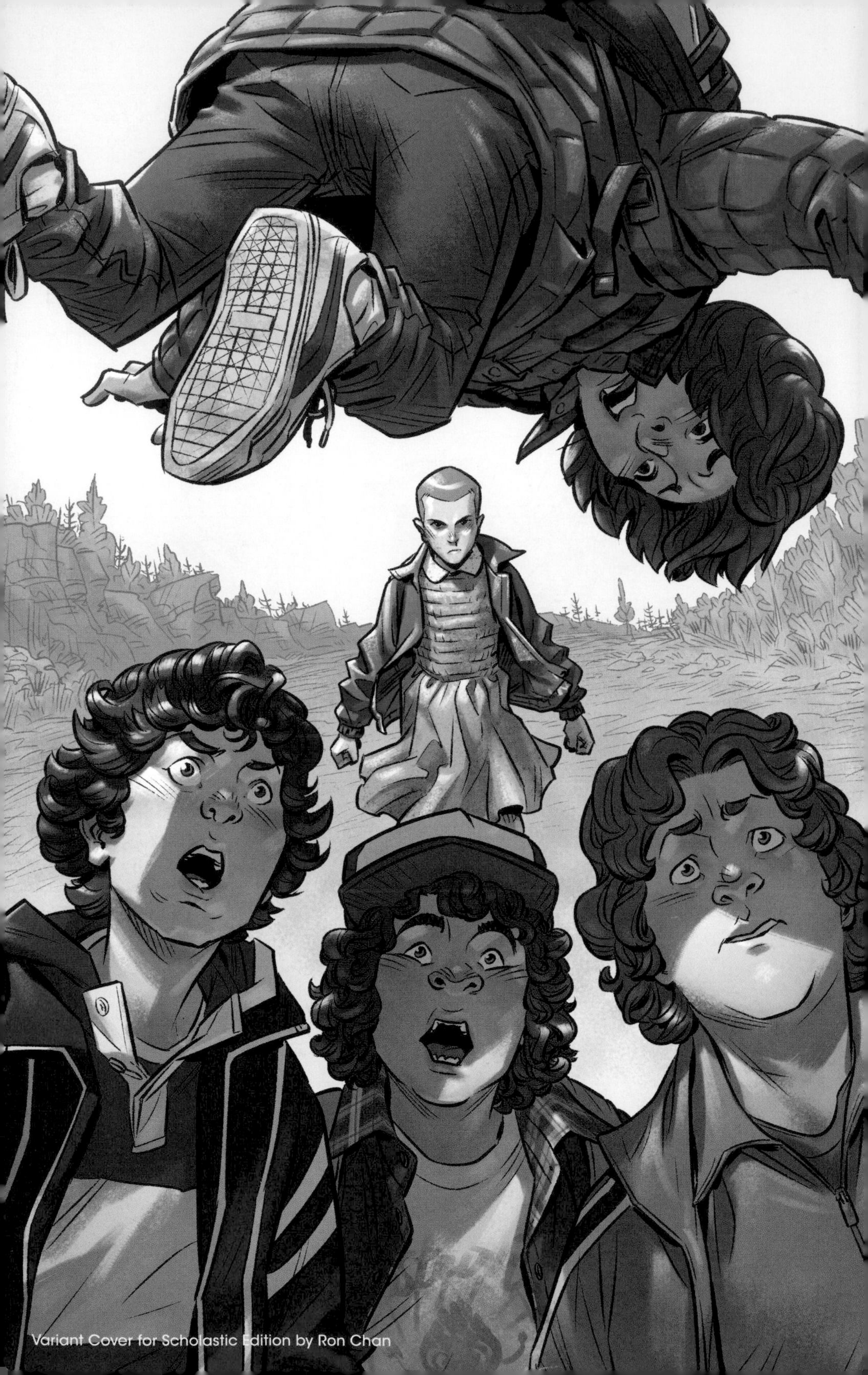

Variant Cover for Scholastic Edition by Ron Chan

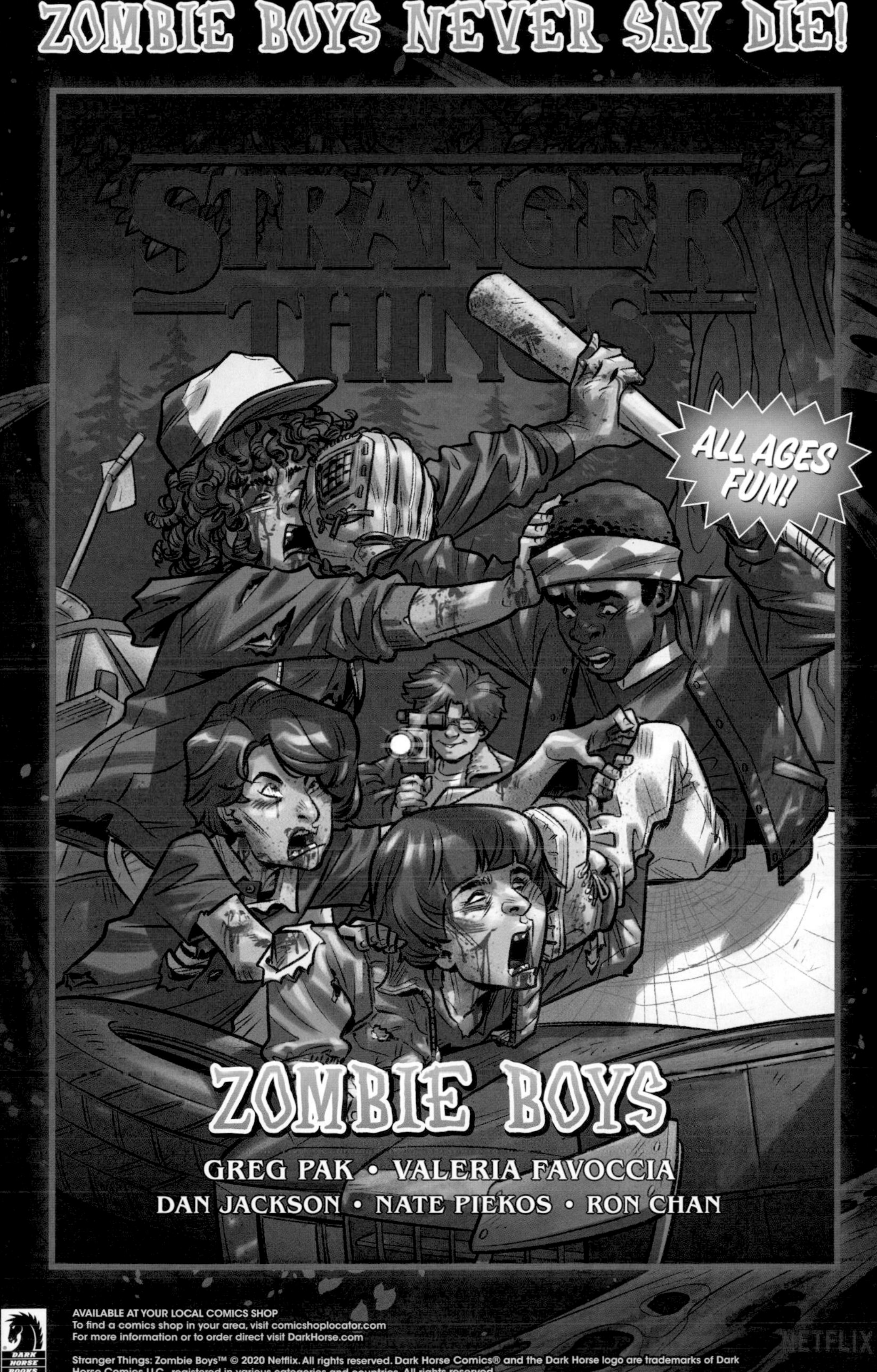
ZOMBIE BOYS NEVER SAY DIE!
STRANGER THINGS
ALL AGES FUN!
ZOMBIE BOYS
GREG PAK • VALERIA FAVOCCIA
DAN JACKSON • NATE PIEKOS • RON CHAN
DARK HORSE BOOKS
AVAILABLE AT YOUR LOCAL COMICS SHOP
To find a comics shop in your area, visit comicshoplocator.com
For more information or to order direct visit DarkHorse.com
NETFLIX
Stranger Things: Zombie Boys™ © 2020 Netflix. All rights reserved. Dark Horse Comics® and the Dark Horse logo are trademarks of Dark Horse Comics LLC, registered in various categories and countries. All rights reserved.

STRANGER THINGS

THE NOSTALGIA-IGNITING HIT NETFLIX ORIGINAL SERIES COMES TO COMICS!

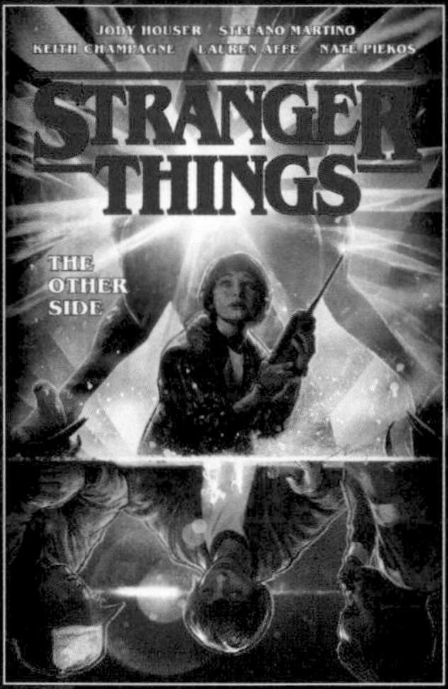

JODY HOUSER STEFANO MARTINO
KEITH CHAMPAGNE LAUREN AFFE NATE PIEKOS
STRANGER THINGS
THE OTHER SIDE

VOLUME 1: THE OTHER SIDE
Jody Houser, Stefano Martino, Keith Champagne, Lauren Affe
ISBN 978-1-50670-976-5
$17.99

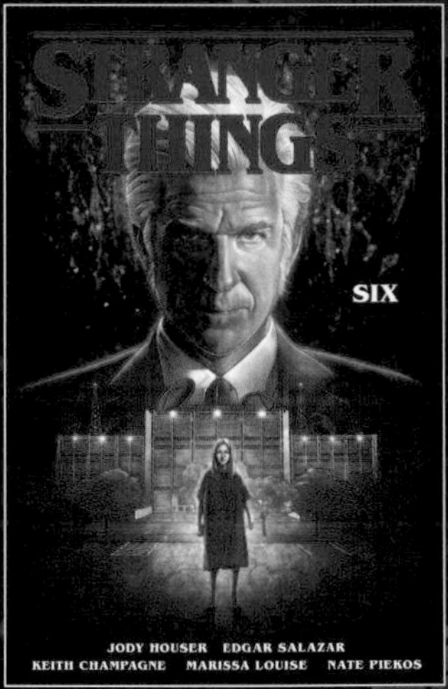

STRANGER THINGS
SIX
JODY HOUSER EDGAR SALAZAR
KEITH CHAMPAGNE MARISSA LOUISE NATE PIEKOS

VOLUME 2: SIX
Jody Houser, Edgar Salazar, Keith Champagne, Marissa Louise
ISBN 978-1-50671-232-1
$17.99

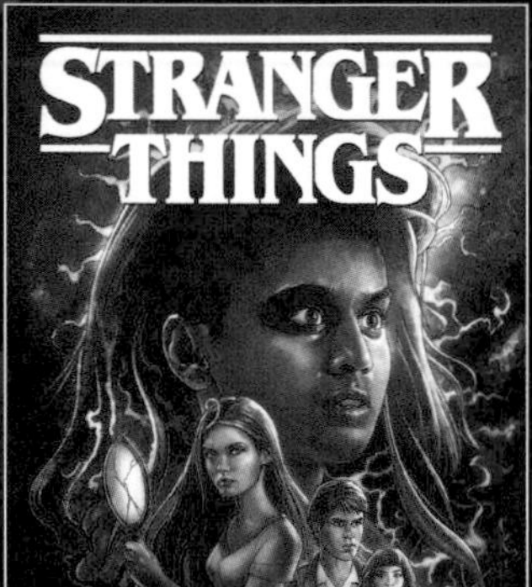

STRANGER THINGS
INTO THE FIRE
JODY HOUSER RYAN KELLY
LE BEAU UNDERWOOD TRIONA FARRELL NATE PIEKOS

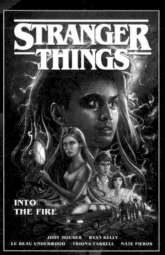

VOLUME 3: INTO THE FIRE
Jody Houser, Ryan Kelly, Le Beau Underwood, Triona Farrell
ISBN 978-1-50671-308-3
$19.99

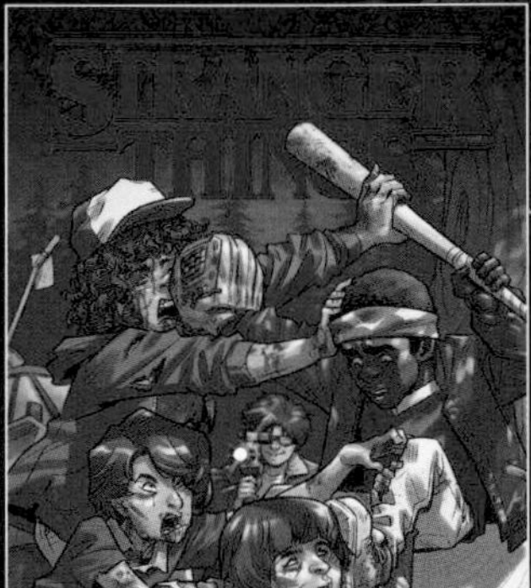

STRANGER THINGS
ZOMBIE BOYS
GREG PAK • VALERIA FAVOCCIA
DAN JACKSON • NATE PIEKOS • RON CHAN

ZOMBIE BOYS
Greg Pak, Valeria Favoccia, Dan Jackson
ISBN 978-1-50671-309-0
$10.99

DARK HORSE COMICS

DARKHORSE.COM • AVAILABLE AT YOUR LOCAL COMICS SHOP OR BOOKSTORE
To find a comics shop near you, visit comicshoplocator.com
For more information or to order direct, visit darkhorse.com

NETFLIX

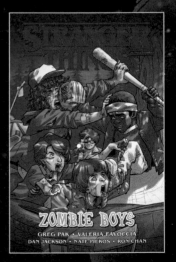